CAMBRIDGE LATIN AMERICAN STUDIES

EDITORS
DAVID JOSLIN   JOHN STREET

2

CHURCH WEALTH IN MEXICO

# THE SERIES

# CHURCH WEALTH IN MEXICO

## A STUDY OF THE 'JUZGADO DE CAPELLANIAS' IN THE ARCHBISHOPRIC OF MEXICO 1800–1856

BY

MICHAEL P. COSTELOE

*Lecturer in the Department of Spanish and Portuguese in the University of Bristol*

CAMBRIDGE

AT THE UNIVERSITY PRESS

1967

Published by the Syndics of the Cambridge University Press
Bentley House, 200 Euston Road, London, N.W. 1
American Branch: 32 East 57th Street, New York, N.Y. 10022

Library of Congress Catalogue Card Number: 67–18310

Printed in Great Britain
at the University Printing House, Cambridge
(Brooke Crutchley, University Printer)

# CONTENTS

# ACKNOWLEDGEMENTS

Grateful acknowledgement is made to the many scholars and the staff of archives and libraries in Great Britain, Mexico and the United States, whose generous assistance and co-operation greatly facilitated the writing of this book. In particular, I am indebted to the University of Newcastle-upon-Tyne to which several chapters were first presented as a doctoral thesis, to Dr N. D. Shergold who supervised and guided my early research, to Professor Woodrow Borah for constant words of encouragement, to Professor Jorge Ignacio Rubio Mañé whose vast knowledge of documentary records in Mexico proved invaluable to me during my stay in that country, and to the editors of this series, Dr J. Street and Professor D. Joslin, for advice and many useful suggestions.

# PREFACE

Ecclesiastical wealth in Mexico became the subject of bitter controversy within a few years of the declaration of independence in 1821. Although both contemporary and recent historians have tried to estimate the total value of clerical holdings of property and capital, and have written much about the effects of so much wealth being owned by one institution, nevertheless, to my knowledge, no detailed study has been made of the way in which the ecclesiastical corporations were able to accumulate their wealth, nor what they did with it once it had reached the coffers of the Church. It is well known, for example, that the Church acted as a type of lending bank, but almost no accurate information has been published concerning the terms of the loan contracts, or the organization responsible for lending the money. Similarly, it is known that the Church gathered tithes, but little is known of the exact way in which the tithe collection system was operated in the nineteenth century. Again, it is agreed that the regular clergy owned much of the urban property in the country, but no details are available of the rental contracts and terms demanded by the Church. Finally, many writers on clerical affairs have mentioned the loans which the Church gave to various independent governments, but no one has examined the way in which such loans were organized, nor made an accurate evaluation of the frequent protestations of the Church that it could not afford to meet the enormous financial demands made upon it by the State.

These and other similar topics have not been investigated, mainly because, even to contemporary scholars like Dr José María Luis Mora and Lucas Alamán, the essential ecclesiastical records have not been accessible. This lack of information has also meant that the many estimates of Church wealth have been based mostly on theoretical calculations, often arranged, in the nineteenth century at least, to suit the political aims of the writer. Fortunately, the records required to study the topics mentioned above have survived in the archdiocese of Mexico. They are housed in the Archivo General de la Nación in Mexico City,

*Preface*

especially in the section entitled Papeles de Bienes Nacionales, which contains almost two thousand bundles of documents, originally taken from the Cathedral archives and the offices of the *Juzgado de Capellanías* in the year 1861 by officials of the Juárez government. They were then apparently deposited in a room in the Secretaría de Hacienda where they remained untouched until some time between 1925 and 1930 when they were removed to their location of today. In 1940 the present director of the Archivo General, Professor Jorge Ignacio Rubio Mañé, began the long, arduous task of sorting and making an inventory of this huge mass of papers, which he completed two years later in 1942.

Armed with the information which this invaluable source provides, I have attempted elsewhere in various articles to investigate some of the topics hitherto neglected, for example tithe administration and Church–State loans. The subject of the present volume is perhaps the most important of all aspects of Church financial interests, that is the organization and lending activities of the *Juzgado de Capellanías*. Because of the breadth and scope of these activities, and also the availability of records, I have restricted my attention to the archbishopric of Mexico. Nevertheless the fiscal administration of the other dioceses was based on similar lines to that of the metropolitan see, which as far as general conclusions are concerned can be taken as broadly typical of the whole country.

Certain points of presentation require explanation. In footnote citations, I have omitted the use of the sign MS, for, unless otherwise stated, all archival references are to manuscripts. The papers in the section Justicia Eclesiástica in the Archivo General are in numbered volumes but they have not been sorted or indexed. I have referred to the volume number and to the page numbers which have only recently been inserted. Finally, it may be of assistance to the reader to know that the standard unit of Mexican currency used in the nineteenth century was the silver peso, which was subdivided into eight reales, one real being equal to twelve granos, and furthermore, that the exchange rate from 1821 until at least 1842 was that of 5 pesos to the £1 sterling.

M. P. C.

# ABBREVIATIONS

ACM  Archivo del Cabildo Metropolitano de México.
AGN  Archivo General de la Nación, Mexico City.
PBN  Papeles de Bienes Nacionales, section of AGN.

# INTRODUCTION

With the declaration of independence in 1821 Mexico looked forward with some justification to a period of advance and development. The nation, freed from the commercial and economic restrictions imposed during the Spanish colonial rule, could now utilize its vast natural resources for its own benefit. With apparently extensive mineral deposits, a rich variety of agricultural produce and large areas of land as yet uncultivated, the future prosperity seemed assured. The new rulers were aware that problems existed and would have to be solved, but in the enthusiasm of victory after the long independence war, few thought that anything could impede the country's progress. Foreign powers took the same view. British merchant interests were foremost in the rush to invest in the declining mining industry, and diplomatic recognition was soon conceded by European nations. In the political sphere, even the debacle of Iturbide's illusionary empire which lasted less than a year did not deter the investors nor dampen the hopes of Mexicans. The establishment of a federal republic in 1824 under the presidency of General Guadalupe Victoria seemed to lay a sound basis for future political stability. In the words of one Mexican recalling these early years, 'Who did not then foresee days of glory, of prosperity and of liberty? Who did not foresee a happy and great future?'[1]

In fact, General Victoria, first president of the Federal Republic, proved to be the only chief executive to complete his term of office for almost the next half century. Until the iron hand of Porfirio Díaz assumed control in 1876, Mexico underwent a period of almost continuous conflict with rebellion, civil war, and foreign intervention destroying the possibilities of progress which had seemed so certain in 1821. There were many causes of this upheaval. The inherent faults of the Spanish colonial society and economy could not be quickly rectified. Too many conflicting interests needed to be satisfied and the nation, with the majority

---

[1] L. de Zavala, *Ensayo histórico de las revoluciones de México, desde 1808 hasta 1830* (Mexico. 1845), vol. I, p. 229.

of its population illiterate peasants, was inevitably dominated by a small oligarchy of articulate and powerful men. The latter were not all self-seeking, ambitious military generals ready to revolt at the first opportunity. Many were intensely preoccupied with the future of their country but almost all sooner or later resorted to the use of force to achieve their ends. There were few alternatives open to them. Military dictators like Santa Anna could not be voted out of office.

The Roman Catholic Church represented one of the principal vested interests seeking to preserve its influence and privileges in the new nation. It had much to defend. There were ten dioceses containing more than one thousand parishes and almost three hundred convents and monasteries.[1] Hospitals, schools, orphanages, and even prisons were managed and financed by ecclesiastical institutions. There were over three thousand priests and four thousand regular clergy to care for the spiritual needs of the people. In the words of one scholar, 'Its enormous economic interests and its control of education, to say nothing of its spiritual hold upon the people, made it dominant in the political and social life of the country'.[2] It is the first of these three points, that is the financial power and influence of the Church, which was of foremost significance during the early decades of independence. The determined efforts of the Church to defend its wealth proved to be one of the indirect causes of much of the great social and political upheaval which took place.

In 1821 the position of the clergy in the young nation seemed secure. There is little doubt that the Church was the richest single corporation in the country, and the prelates controlled a vast organization which extended to every corner of the land, and whose influence was felt in every sphere. The clergy, not unnaturally, expected to play an active part in both the secular and religious life of the nation. In the colonial era, the Church had exercised considerable political power and had formed an

[1] The most reliable account of the numbers of clergy and clerical institutions of all kinds is the *Libro de inscripción del Ven. Clero Mexicano en el año de 1851*, by Archbishop Lázaro de la Garza. It is in the Archivo General de la Nación, Mexico City, section Papeles de Bienes Nacionales (cited hereinafter as AGN, PBN), leg. 127, exp. 2.

[2] W. H. Callcott, *Church and State in Mexico, 1822–1857* (Durham, N. Carolina, 1926), p. 4.

2

additional arm of government on behalf of the Crown, even to the extent that several prelates had acted as temporary or permanent viceroy with full judicial and military authority. Moreover, in spite of such precedent, other factors now determined the intervention of the clergy in civil and, especially, in political activity. It was realized that, with royal protection removed and the once-powerful Inquisition abolished, the Church was clearly susceptible to attack from the exponents of the heretical liberal philosophy which was spreading so quickly in Europe, and whose origins had in part provided the stimulus to the emancipation movement in Latin America. The clergy, to safeguard not only the faith, but also their wealth, needed to achieve a position in which they could influence if not control governmental policy and action.

The need to achieve this position led in part to the dispute over the royal patronage.[1] Patronage over the Church had been the prerogative of the Spanish monarchy throughout the colonial period and had given the civil authority almost complete jurisdiction over the activities of the ecclesiastical corporations. Shiels has summarized the extent of the royal control as follows:

Under the *patronato real*, all funds for the support of religion became by a fiction of law government moneys, to be dispensed by the administration in Madrid or by its subordinate viceroys, who gave approval and direction to every major religious activity. All religious corporations looked directly to the court for authorizations, permissions, subventions, or judgment of pleas. The crown held the nomination of bishops, canons, parish priests, the erection of convents, colleges, welfare associations, and the conceding of the *pase regio* to all indulgences, privileges, and pontifical bulls.[2]

With the separation from Spain achieved, both the Church and the new State claimed the right to exercise the patronage, the clergy declaring that with the removal of the monarchy as the

---

[1] The patronage problem has been ably studied by W. E. Shiels, *King and Church. The Rise and Fall of the Patronato Real* (Chicago, 1961). I have based the following summary of the problem as regards Mexico on an earlier article by the same author: 'Church and State in the first decade of Mexican independence.' *Catholic Historical Review*, XXVIII (July 1942), 206–28.

[2] Shiels, 'Church and State', 208.

civil power, the privileges originally conceded by the papacy ceased, and the new independence governments maintaining that the patronage devolved upon them as the successors to the Crown.

No solution could be found immediately because of the major political implications in the European sphere and especially in the papal relations with Spain. Protracted negotiations were initiated with Rome but these were to last for many years. In the meantime, the Church found itself unable to reconstitute its own episcopal hierarchy, for no new senior ecclesiastical appointments could be made until the correct nominating body had been decided upon. As a result the shortage of clergy which inevitably followed the long war in which many were killed and others had returned to Spain became acute, not only among the lower ranks but also among the episcopate. In 1822 there were only four bishops out of a possible total of ten, and it was not until after 1836, when relations were formally re-established with Spain, that all the vacant sees were filled. The Church, from the point of view of numbers of clergy and senior spokesmen, found itself weaker and weaker at the very time in which it was to come under attack. Clerical determination and persistence over the patronage problem was partly pursued in the hope that the Church would be able to strengthen its position by achieving for the first time almost complete autonomy and freedom from the civil authority.

_The desire of the clergy to safeguard and fortify their own position proved to be well founded, for within a few years of independence an increasing number of men of radical views began to make their voices heard in public affairs. They were mostly of liberal opinions, and to them the clergy represented a privileged minority group, whose primary allegiance was not to the State but to the Church, and who consequently put the good of the Church before the good of the nation. In order to avoid a theocratic State it was essential that the Church should be made subject to and responsible to the civil government. Furthermore, the juridical and fiscal autonomy of the Church recalled the colonial regime in which individual liberty had long been restricted by corporate privilege. They attacked clerical participation in secular affairs, especially education, charging that

4

the Church had failed to provide an adequate educational system, partly because in matters of curriculum the clergy continued to teach antiquated subjects and attitudes, and partly because facilities for instruction were available only to a very small part of the population. Finally, and of the greatest implication, they began to advocate the appropriation and nationalization of ecclesiastical property and capital on the economic grounds that this wealth should and could be made more productive and beneficial to the public good.

The clergy well realized the threat to the Church caused by such radical and, to them, heretical views, and allied with the conservative elements in society they strenuously resisted any proposed change in their status or encroachment on their goods. They were able to maintain their defence for almost four decades, largely as a result, not only of their spiritual influence, but also of their enormous financial power. Ecclesiastical corporations soon began to give their monetary support to those administrations which proposed no alteration in clerical affairs, and at least in one instance, the Polko revolt of 1847, the Church actively encouraged and financed a military rebellion against a liberal administration which was threatening its property. This intervention in the political sphere and the use of ecclesiastical funds to prevent any clerical reform, brought the liberals to the conclusion that their own survival depended largely on the Church, for it was clear that the clergy would tolerate no administration which threatened their goods.

The attitude of the State towards Church wealth underwent certain changes and development after 1821. The liberal argument was basically that appropriation and nationalization were required for economic reasons, and to this they soon added the financial needs of the national government. The conservatives, on the other hand, naturally refused to accept this view, and in the first decade of independence they resisted all pressures to force the clergy to part with their goods. After the defeat of the liberals' attempted reform in 1833, the attitude of both sides changed. The fiscal position of the nation became so critical that even the conservatives and pro-clerical administrations found that they were increasingly obliged to demand monetary assistance from the Church. The liberals now to some extent abandoned their economic argument and concentrated on more immediate needs. By 1856, when they began their final and successful assault on Church wealth, they did not pursue this for economic and social motives. In the words of one scholar, 'The *Ley Lerdo* and the laws of 1859, concerned primarily with the disentailment of Church property, did not undertake "the restructuring of the social classes nor the deconcentration of lay property". The aim was rather political—further removal of the Church from a position of power—and financial, to increase government resources and to secure foreign loans.'[1]

Apart from the general principles of the liberal philosophy concerning the place of the Church in society, an attack on Church wealth was in several respects inevitable, because of the anomalous situation which began in 1821 and continued until 1856, that is, a rich Church and an impoverished government. In 1821 the economy of the country was in ruins. The previous years of war had their inevitable effects on commerce, agriculture, and industry, and with independence achieved many of the educated and richer Spaniards, who in the colonial period had supplied virtually every administrative official, returned to Spain, taking with them both their skill and their capital. Furthermore, the nation inherited an internal debt which in 1821 was estimated to stand at 76,286,499 pesos.[2] It was not, however, the moment for austerity and the early governments saw fit to lower taxes and trust that the great natural resources of the country would be developed and that the economic situation would improve. On 5, 7, 12 October, 22 November and 15 December 1821, taxes were either abolished or reduced. The total revenue of the government soon showed an alarming decline. In 1810, according to Alamán, it had amounted to 6,455,422 pesos. By 1822 this had dropped to only 1,348,170 pesos and expenditure totalled more than 4,000,000.[3] Voluntary and forced loans were decreed but neither met with much success. It

---

[1] C. A. Hale, 'José María Luis Mora and the structure of Mexican liberalism', *Hispanic American Historical Review*, XLV (May 1965), 213.

[2] L. Alamán, *Historia de México desde los primeros movimientos que prepararon su independencia en el año de 1808 hasta la época presente* (México, 1852), vol. V, p. 433.

[3] Alamán, V, 422.

soon became imperative to find a large and steady supply of money with which to maintain and run the government.

The Church was the only institution in the country that seemed in a position to raise the large amounts of capital that were needed, and, although this fact was well realized, no thought or attempt at general confiscation of clerical property was yet considered. This was due to some extent to the fact that as early as 1822 the clergy had already begun to exercise political influence, and in 1824 the General Congress decreed that no changes were to be introduced in the present administration of ecclesiastical revenues.[1] Successive Ministers of Justice and Ecclesiastical Affairs emphasized the decline in the wealth of the Church that had taken place during the previous two decades. In 1826 the Minister estimated that Church revenue had decreased by half,[2] and in the same year the clergy themselves produced a detailed report to show that the convents in the Federal District were not as rich as was generally thought.[3] In 1824 rumours had begun to spread that the government was preparing a wholesale confiscation of the property and possessions of the convents. The state governor hastened to reassure the clergy and a circular was issued which denied that any such action was contemplated.[4]

The government, therefore, unwilling to confiscate clerical wealth and thereby raise the needed funds from within the nation, decided to seek financial aid from abroad. Mexican government bonds were sold in London, and the interest and capital repayment of these was guaranteed by mortgaging the customs at Vera Cruz and the revenue of several state monopolies, with the result that the regular income to the government was even further reduced.[5] The annual budget deficits during this period were calculated by the Minister of Hacienda in 1870. He estimated

---

[1] Shiels states that in the 1822 elections, Mexico City returned a preponderance of clergy to Congress; Shiels, 'Church and State', p. 211.

[2] *Memoria del Ministro de Justicia y Negocios Eclesiásticos* (1826), p. 15.

[3] *Noticia individual comprensiva de todos los conventos de religiosas del Arzobispado de México ... formado de orden del ilustrísimo y venerable señor Deán y Cabildo, Gobernador de la expresada diocesis, por su vicario el Dr. D. Juan Bautista de Arechederreta, en el mes de mayo del año de 1826:* publ. in *Boletín del Archivo General de la Nación,* XXIV (1953), 473–7.

[4] The circular and documents concerning this are in AGN, PBN, leg. 134, exp. 9.

[5] Details of these loans are given in Callcott, *Church and State*, pp. 51–2.

that in 1825 the deficit reached 7,296,000 pesos, and that by 1831 this had risen to 8,499,680 pesos.[1] No further support could be solicited from foreign bankers, for the government had been unable to meet repayments on the loans already contracted. The foreign debt stood at 34,287,750 pesos, including the accrued interests that had not been paid.[2] In spite of various fiscal manœuvres and agreements reached with the bondholders during the following two decades, Mexican credit was not to be restored in Europe, with the exception of a brief interlude during the Maximilian government, until the advent of the Díaz regime and its encouragement of foreign investment. Hence there being no possibility of raising funds abroad, the attention of the treasury ministers was drawn to within the country, and the wealth of the Church was clearly an anomaly that would sooner or later come under attack.

Within a few years of independence, clerical wealth began to be considered from another viewpoint which was not directly connected with the immediate fiscal needs of the government. The growth of this coincides with the rise to prominence of the liberals, particularly in the state of Zacatecas. The liberals came to the conclusion that the possession of so much of the nation's capital and property in the hands of one corporation was hindering the country's economic progress. It was also thought that the riches of the various corporations within the Church could be employed in a more productive manner. In particular, to men like Dr José María Luis Mora, who became the main liberal critic of Church wealth, the regular orders seemed to serve no useful purpose of any kind, and even impartial observers like the British representative H. G. Ward thought that some reform was clearly necessary.[3] Signs of this new attitude appeared in several states.

In 1824 the congress of Jalisco tried to assume the administration of all clerical revenue within the State,[4] and two years later in 1826, a law was passed in Durango which ordered the confiscation

---

[1] The table giving the Minister's calculations is quoted in J. Sierra, *México. Su evolución social* (Mexico, 1902), vol. II, p. 370.

[2] Alamán, v, 956.

[3] H. G. Ward, *Mexico in 1827* (London, 1828), vol. I, pp. 347–8.

[4] E. Galarza, *The Roman Catholic Church as a Factor in the Political and Social History of Mexico* (Sacramento, 1928), p. 85.

of certain clerical funds which were to be used to finance an irrigation scheme.[1] In 1827 the State of Mexico considered taking over the collection of tithes[2] and this was followed in 1828 by a more significant proposal. On 7 December 1828 the congress of Zacatecas passed provisionally a law by which all the property and possessions of the pious works, for example, funds destined for religious festivals, charities, and schools, were to be appropriated to provide capital for the foundation of an agricultural bank, which would pay the Church 5 per cent interest on the confiscated funds. Also a third part of the revenue from tithes was to be given to the bank. Naturally the clergy from all over the country made strong representations against the proposal, which was eventually abandoned.[3] Nevertheless, this and earlier attempts at confiscation or control of clerical revenue and goods are significant in that they seem to have been inspired, not solely by the financial poverty of the state governments, but also by more general economic needs, for it was thought that the wealth of the Church could be better employed. The following year, 1829, the congress of Chihuahua tried to take over the administration of all clerical possessions, including the tithes, and to abolish the parochial dues.[4]

By about 1830, therefore, Church wealth was clearly in danger for two reasons; first the financial needs of the government, and secondly, the increasing opinion that clerical riches could be made more productive. The only problem concerned the question of whether the State had the right to appropriate the legally acquired possessions of the Church. Confiscation could be justified on the grounds of precedent, for the Spanish monarchs, with the consent of the clergy, had appropriated large amounts of ecclesiastical capital when the Crown found itself in financial need. The expulsion of the Jesuit Order in 1767 caused the first

[1] *Colección eclesiástica mexicana* (Mexico, 1834), vol. IV, pp. 3–5.

[2] Clerical opposition resulted in this idea being abandoned; see *Exposición del Cabildo Metropolitano al Honorable Congreso del Estado de México*, 26 May 1827, AGN, *Justicia Eclesiástica*, vol. 67, fols. 193 ff.

[3] A copy of the law and the clerical representations against it are in AGN, *Justicia Eclesiástica*, vol. 97, fols. 65–106.

[4] Two laws dated 28 September 1829. A copy of both and pleas for their repeal are in AGN, *Justicia Eclesiástica*, vol. 87, fols. 98 ff.

major confiscation and the goods which were then taken over
provided a source of revenue to governments until at least 1829.[1]
In 1798, with the Spanish treasury almost bankrupt, a royal
decree introduced a direct tax on clerical investments. Further
special war taxes were levied and then on 26 December 1804 a
royal decree ordered the implementation of the laws of consolidation.[2] These required that all the invested capital from benefices
and pious works should be withdrawn from circulation and
placed in the royal coffers. In spite of such precedents, however,
the liberal politicians in Zacatecas decided to seek a definitive
answer to the problem and announced that a prize would be
given for the best dissertation on a topic which was, briefly, the
right of the State to confiscate clerical property. The winning
entry, which was published soon afterwards, was submitted by
Dr Mora, who came to the conclusion that the State was fully
entitled to nationalize the possessions of the Church.[3]

It was clear, therefore, that when the liberals, headed by Vice-
President Gómez Farías, came to power in 1833, they would
introduce measures to reduce Church wealth. In fact they did
not concentrate solely on this but first tried to decrease clerical
influence in other spheres. A series of laws was passed: the clergy
were forbidden to make political speeches, all missions were
secularized, the University of Mexico, long dominated by the
clergy, was closed, and a Department of Public Education was
set up, the regular clergy were allowed to renounce their vows,
and the civil obligation to pay tithes was abolished.[4] The major
liberal proposals concerning clerical wealth never became law.
Although considerations of economic and political benefit were
clearly prominent, the immediate justification for the proposed
confiscations was claimed to be the fiscal need of the nation.
Consequently, on 20 November 1833 Dr Mora published an

[1] *Estado de las fincas urbanas y rústicas respectivas a las temporalidades de los ecs-jesuitas y monacales suprimidas, con expresión de sus valores, gravamen que reportan y renta anual* (Mexico, 1829).

[2] The effects of the consolidation laws are discussed in chapter 5.

[3] J. M. L. Mora, *Disertación sobre la naturaleza y aplicación de las rentas y bienes eclesiásticos* (Mexico, 1833). I have used a later edition published in Mexico, 1957.

[4] The liberals also declared that the patronage was and had been an inherent right of the nation: Shiels, 'Church and State', p. 228.

## Introduction

article in the newspaper *Indicador de la Federación* in which he considered possible ways of reducing the internal public debt.[1] His main suggestion was that the government should do this by appropriating ecclesiastical goods. A few months later, on 17 February 1834, a report from the Commission on Public Credit was presented to the Congress.[2] This also recommended that the wealth of the Church should be used to amortize the public debt.

These proposals and laws, with the notable exception of the one concerning tithes, were never effectively implemented because of the hostile reaction of the conservative and pro-clerical supporters. The liberals were soon struggling to retain power, and there seems little doubt that the clergy were lending their moral and financial support to the several revolutions which broke out. Eventually the attitude of Santa Anna determined the success of the conservatives and Church, and the liberals were defeated. The Church had survived the first major assault on its wealth.

The defeat of the attempted reform of 1833–4 and the subsequent establishment of a centralist and pro-clerical government in 1835 did not alter the basic financial position of the nation. This remained precarious and was to grow worse over the next decade until by 1845 the estimated deficit had risen to more than fourteen million pesos.[3] Under such circumstances, even the conservative administrations began to demand that the Church should part with some of its goods. The usual method adopted for achieving this was to ask the Church to lend money to the government, and in most cases the clergy agreed. Lending money to the civil authorities was not in fact a new practice for the Church. During the colonial period many loans had been given to the Spanish monarchs, and in the period 1792 to 1812 the sum of 675,172 pesos had been handed over for a variety of purposes.[4]

[1] The main points of this article are reproduced in J. M. L. Mora, *El clero, el estado y la economía nacional*, ed. M. L. Guzmán (Mexico, 1950), pp. 137–49: this volume is no. xv in the collection entitled *El liberalismo mexicano en pensamiento y en acción*.
[2] Sections of this report are published in the above volume, pp. 205–13.
[3] *Memoria del Ministro de Hacienda* (1870).
[4] Account made by the Tithe Accountant's Office, 15 October 1812, Archivo del Cabildo Metropolitano de México (hereinafter referred to as ACM), vol. entitled *Expedientes, comunicaciones*, etc. 1796–1814. These loans were mostly of small amounts to help in the purchase of such items as shoes, clothing, and weapons, etc., for the military.

Many loans were given to the viceregal authorities during the war of independence, for example, on 11 December 1811 a meeting was held between the Viceroy and two clerical representatives, Dr D. Pedro de Fonte and Dr Andrés Fernández de Madrid, which resulted in a loan of 252,548 pesos being given by the Church.[1]

Apart from numerous direct loans, conservative Ministers began to devise other schemes to persuade the clergy to give up at least some of their wealth. In 1838 the Minister of Hacienda, Manuel Gorostiza, outlined a new project. He suggested the establishment of a bank and he published a project entitled: 'Project of a law for the foundation of a "Patriotic Bank" of the Mexican Clergy.'[2] The terms of the foundation were to allow the clergy to establish a bank with a capital of eight million pesos. The bank was to provide finance for commerce, industry, and agriculture. An immediate loan of six million pesos was to be given to the government and a savings branch was to be set up, paying an annual interest of 6 per cent. The bank would be directed by several representatives of the clergy and three government officials. The clergy saw no advantage to the Church in this proposal and refused to give their support, and as a result no further action was taken.

Hence by 1846 when the war with the United States of America began, it was inevitable, regardless of the political ideals of the government in power, that Church wealth would have to be utilized. In fact the liberals gained office in this period and they quickly turned their attention to the Church.[3] Their demands now seemed based entirely on the problems arising from the war. The most important of these was the need for cash with which to pay and equip the armed forces, and clerical riches were the obvious source. On this occasion the liberals were able to and did maintain that their proposed confiscation of Church property was

---

[1] *Expediente formado sobre la recaudación del Préstamo abierto por la Hacienda Pública en el año de 1811*, ACM, vol. 62.

[2] Minister of *Hacienda* to Minister of Interior, 24 April 1838, AGN, *Justicia Eclesiástica*, vol. 127, fol. 299. The replies of the clergy to the proposal are also in this volume.

[3] For an account of the fiscal dealings which took place at this time, see my article 'Church–State financial negotiations in Mexico during the American war, 1846–1847', *Revista de Historia de América*, vol. 60 (June–December 1965).

based on nothing more than the immediate financial requirements caused by the war. It is impossible to ascertain exactly the reasons behind the law of 11 January 1847, whereby Gómez Farías, supported by a liberal majority in Congress, proposed the confiscation of clerical goods to the value of fifteen million pesos. Farías and his Ministers tried to justify the measure on the grounds of desperate fiscal crisis, but it seems likely that they also realized that this presented the opportunity of carrying out, under the pretext of the national emergency, their previously declared policy of dispossessing the Church of its goods, and thereby removing a major cause of its political influence. This possibility, indeed probability, also occurred to the Church leaders, who constantly refused to accept the anti-clerical legislation, in spite of threats and appeals to them on humanitarian and patriotic grounds. A massive propaganda campaign against the law was raised in the press, and when this appeared to be failing, the clergy resorted to direct military opposition. The rebellion of the Polkos, which began on the night of 26 February 1847, was engineered and financed by the ecclesiastical corporations in the capital. The aims of this rebellion were the annulment of the confiscation laws and the removal from office of the liberal leader, Gómez Farías, and although these were not won directly by military means, they were quickly achieved. Santa Anna, faced with revolutions in the capital and other parts of the country, soon realized that the Church could not at that time be forced to part with its possessions. Hence he reached a compromise with the clergy whereby, in return for a loan, he in effect dismissed Farías and revoked the liberal legislation.[1]

The events of 1847 had again vividly illustrated to the liberals that their own political future depended on removing the power and wealth of the Church, and it is not surprising that when they returned to office a few years later they again pursued the same policy which they had failed to implement in 1833 and in 1847. The publication of the *Ley Juárez* on 23 November 1855 signalled the beginning of the final stage in the liberal assault on the

[1] For details of clerical intervention in this rebellion, see my article 'The Mexican Church and the rebellion of the Polkos', *Hispanic American Historical Review*, XLVI (May 1966), 170–8.

Church and its wealth, and civil war inevitably followed. The subsequent military victory of the liberals finally enabled them to carry out the measures that had been formulated almost thirty years earlier, and all clerical property and capital were nationalized.

It is clear, therefore, that Church wealth was one of the key issues in the political development of independent Mexico and especially in the rise to power of the new class of progressive radicals. From the long-term view Church wealth was of even greater significance in the economic sphere, for it was in this that the clergy had their greatest influence in the temporal and secular affairs of the nation. The liberals' objection to ecclesiastical riches was essentially based on the harm they caused to agricultural and industrial development, and they envisaged a kind of economic emancipation resulting from the nationalization of clerical property and capital. As we have seen, however, more immediate financial and political needs determined their actions. Nevertheless, it was in the field of economic development that the clergy exercised their greatest influence. They were able to achieve this position and accumulate their great wealth because of a number of circumstances.

In many respects it was inevitable that the Church would acquire great wealth in Mexico and that the State would eventually have to intervene and nationalize clerical holdings of real estate and capital. The main purpose of the conquest and colonization of New Spain was in theory the conversion of the indigenous population to the Christian faith, which meant that the clergy were looked upon from the very beginning as key members of the colonial society. The privileges enjoyed by the Church in Spain, for example the ecclesiastical *fuero*, were therefore naturally transferred to the newly established Church in Mexico. In addition, apart from religious conviction, the Spanish monarchs were well aware of the value of an established Church in maintaining their own influence and control over the distant colony. It was in the interest of the Crown to encourage and protect the development of a powerful Church. Consequently the tithes were given to the clergy, and while these were considered to provide insufficient revenue, a royal subsidy was added. Throughout the sixteenth century the regular clergy were allowed to consolidate and extend their wealth, and in spite of popular appeals against the increasing size of their possessions the Spanish monarchs made no real effort to prevent their continuous acquisition of property and capital.

Apart from royal protection, two other factors combined to enable the Church to acquire more and more riches. First, there is no doubt that the majority of the population were firm believers in the Roman Catholic religion, and although complaints against the financial activities of the Church were made from time to time, most people continued to give their support to the Church, either by way of gifts or by establishing pious works and ecclesiastical benefices. With the exception of forced labour exacted from the indigenous races and of the tithes which in the sixteenth and seventeenth centuries did not yield a great amount of revenue, all other material possessions acquired by the clerical corporations were the result of voluntary offerings on the part of the population, though no doubt some priests did coerce their parishioners into making bequests to the Church. Nevertheless, with only one minor exception, the individual citizen was not obliged by law to give or bequeath anything to the Church.[1]

The second factor conducive to the wealth of the Church lay in the clergy themselves. The internal organization of the Church in New Spain was not new and untried but was a transplantation of the administrative system that had been developed in Spain over a long period and under the guidance of the central authority in Rome. The higher ranks of the clergy who were sent to the new colony, in addition to being the best educated section in society, were experienced in fiscal matters and well versed in the ways and methods of managing holdings of real estate and utilizing capital to the best advantage. Their education and experience enabled them to develop the internal fiscal organization of the Church in accordance with the methods and principles which had proved to

[1] The one exception was the *mandas forzosas*. Every person making a will was obliged to bequeath a sum of money to certain pious works, but the amount was left to the decision of the individual, and usually only a few *reales* were given. Most of the *mandas forzosas* were established by royal decree in the eighteenth century but they were still being observed after independence; for example, see the wills in AGN, PBN, leg. 743, exp. 1; 896/7, 124/5.

be successful in Spain. As a result, such ecclesiastical benefices as the *capellanía* and the pious work were encouraged in the newly founded Church, and ideas regarding the investment of capital and acquisition of real estate were quickly discussed, with due attention paid to the conditions existent in New Spain. Ecclesiastical councils were held in 1555, 1565, and 1585 in which attempts were made to formulate definite fiscal policies.[1] Gradually, administrative organizations evolved to manage the ever-increasing riches.

Church wealth came from three main sources and each affected a specific sector of the economy.[2] The first of these was the tithes which resulted from a tax on agricultural production.[3] The right to levy these was granted to the Crown in a papal bull of 1 January 1501, the intention being that the revenue collected should be used by the monarch towards financing the establishment of the Church, and towards providing a stipend for the clergy. Spaniards and mestizos, and to a lesser extent the Indians, were expected to pay, and virtually every item of produce, from cows and sheep to eggs and milk, was taxable, and not even the parish priests themselves were exempt. The distribution of the money raised from the sale of the produce was made in accordance with royal decrees issued on 3 October 1539, 6 July 1540, and 15 February 1541. The basic division was as follows: one quarter was given to the bishop, and one quarter to the Cathedral chapter; the remaining half was divided into ninths, four of which went to the parishes, three to the maintenance of ecclesiastical buildings and hospitals, and the remaining two ninths were reserved for the monarch. This theoretical division remained without alteration until the year 1804 when an additional ninth was ordered to be

[1] For example, decisions were taken on real estate investment; M. Galván Rivera, *Concilio III Mexicano, celebrado en México el año de 1585* (Mexico, 1859), p. 250.

[2] I omit three minor sources of revenue. First, the parochial dues, because this money did not become an integral part of the overall clerical wealth in that it was spent by the individual priests as it was received, and no part of it reached the communal coffers of the Church. Secondly and thirdly, first fruits and alms are disregarded because neither was a permanent or constant source of revenue, and both seem to have yielded only negligible amounts in the nineteenth century.

[3] I have discussed the tithes in more detail in 'The administration, collection, and distribution of tithes in the archbishopric of Mexico, 1800–1860', *The Americas*, xxiii (July, 1966), 3–27.

set aside for the Crown. This was subtracted from the gross amount and then the previous division was carried out on the remainder.

By the end of the eighteenth century the tithes had become a rich source of income to the Church and a large administrative organization had evolved to arrange the collection and distribution of the tax. Humboldt calculated that from 1771 to 1780 the yield in the metropolitan diocese alone amounted to more than four million pesos, and in the following decade this increased to more than seven million.[1] His figures are supported by other accounts, one of which reveals that in 1792 the tax yielded 729,719 pesos.[2] The rise did not continue after the turn of the century. According to an account found among the records of the metropolitan chapter, the average yield for the years 1806 to 1810 was 510,081 pesos, which represents a drop of almost 30 per cent on the 1792 figure.[3] Then the long war of independence which followed caused an even more rapid decline. Agricultural production inevitably decreased and often crops were stolen or destroyed by the rampaging armies before the tithe collectors could make any assessment or claim on behalf of the Church. Indeed, one account reveals that during the war of independence almost half of the collection districts into which the archbishopric was divided were at one time so badly damaged that they yielded no revenue, and that all of the others suffered considerable loss through theft.[4] The only account book that has survived from this period shows that by 1821, the year of independence, the tithe revenue in the archdiocese had dropped to approximately 233,000 pesos, that is less than one third of the amount at the end of the eighteenth century.[5] It is reasonable to assume that the other bishoprics suffered a similar decrease.

[1] A. von Humboldt, *Political Essay on the Kingdom of New Spain* (London, 1811), vol. III, p. 96.
[2] *Extracto de la cuenta de diezmos de la Santa Iglesia de México del año entero de mil setecientos noventa y dos...*, dated September 2, 1793, AGN, *Diezmos*, vol 20.
[3] *Noticia de lo que han producido los diezmos del Arzobispado de México en los diversos quinquenios para deducir por ellos el cálculo aproximado de lo que rendirán en lo sucesivo los de todas las Iglesias de la República en el caso de que se derogue la ley de 27 de octubre de 1833*, ACM, vol. 63.
[4] *Productos líquidos que daban las siguientes colecturías antes de que quedasen enteramente destruidas por los insurgentes*, undated, ACM, vol. 62.
[5] *Libro de colectores que da principio con las cuentas de diezmos de 1816*, ACM.

The next decade saw little improvement in the position. Again the metropolitan diocese vividly illustrates the situation. In 1833 the tithes produced less than 140,000 pesos.[1] It was in this year that the liberals began their first major assault on the wealth of the Church and on 27 October a law was issued which abolished the civil obligation to pay tithes.[2] This had an immediate effect and collectors from all parts of the archbishopric reported that people were refusing to pay.[3] In 1834 the annual yield dropped to less than 90,000 pesos and the decline continued.[4] Almost twenty years later the *Jueces Hacedores*, directors of the tithe organization, reported to the prelate that nothing had been collected in some areas since 1833.[5] The account books of the collectors graphically confirm this statement. Each page in these books was reserved for a particular farm or property within the area covered by the collector. Before 1833 every page was covered with details of the total produce of the farm and the amount paid in tithes. After 1833 most pages are blank except for the collector's comment that the person involved had refused to pay.[6]

Every effort was made by the ecclesiastical officials to remedy the situation. Priests were urged to remind their parishioners of their religious obligations and various committees were established to seek means of making the administration and collection system more economic. Changes were made in the districts in an attempt to cut operating costs, the number of employees was reduced, and several new sets of regulations were devised.[7] Such measures

[1] *Libro de colectores que da principio con las cuentas de diezmos de 1816*, ACM.
[2] M. Dublán y J. M. Lozano, *Legislación mexicana* (Mexico, 1876), vol. II, p. 577.
[3] See, for example, letter inside the *Cuenta de la colecturía de diezmos de Huejutla*, 1840, ACM.
[4] *Libro de colectores*, 1816, ACM.
[5] Report of *Jueces Hacedores* to Archbishop, 9 October 1852, AGN, PBN, leg. 1524, exp. 135.
[6] Many of these account books have survived and are now in the chapter archive in the Cathedral; for a description of the contents of this archive, see my 'Guide to the chapter archives of the archbishopric of Mexico', *Hispanic American Historical Review*, XLV (February 1965), 53–63.
[7] Two new sets of regulations to govern the organization of the tithe collection system were introduced in 1845 and 1846: *Reglamento para la intervención, aprobada por el illmo. sr. Arzobispo y su venerable cabildo en el celebrado en 29 de julio de 1845: Reglamento a que deberán sujetarse los colectores de la Santa Iglesia de México, acordado por el illmo. sr. Arzobispo y su venerable sr. Deán y cabildo en el celebrado en 11 de febrero de 1846*. There are printed copies of these regulations in ACM. Also there is a copy of the former in AGN, PBN, leg. 327, exp. 26.

were of no avail, and after 1833 what had formerly been the Church's greatest source of income was in effect abolished.

There is little doubt that the tithes were an unpopular levy and were widely considered to be detrimental to the development of agriculture. In 1809 the *Jueces Hacedores* reported that those people responsible for paying the tax in the archbishopric made every effort to avoid doing so.[1] Resentment and opposition were to be expected, at least on the grounds that the levy was discriminatory in that it was only imposed on those people involved in agricultural production. It was an unfair burden on the farmer and even Bishop Abad y Queipo, writing in 1805 in defence of the Church, acknowledged this fact.[2] It is not surprising that many people availed themselves of the law of 1833 and stopped payment. It is also of interest to note that in spite of constant appeals and threats on religious and other grounds, and the deployment of the influence of local priests on their parishioners, most former payers steadfastly refused to pay. This fact is even more significant if one takes into account the comprehensive organization of the collection system under which information on every property and farmer was known to the clerical officials. Even the combined pressure of the latter and the priests was not sufficient. It seems likely that the law of 1833 was one liberal measure welcomed by the majority of the population.

The abolition of tithes, however, had other implications and effects. The liberals must have attached great weight to it from the economic viewpoint, for it adversely affected themselves in two ways. In the first place, the people who suffered most from tithes were the landowners, the majority of whom were conservatives who opposed most of the policy advocated by the liberals. The latter, therefore, by abolishing the tithes, indirectly aided their political opponents, presumably in the belief that the long-term advantages to agriculture justified the measure. In the circumstances prevalent in 1833 another consideration was perhaps of even greater importance. The tithe was by that time not strictly an

---

[1] *Jueces Hacedores* to *Fiscal de lo Civil*, 17 August 1809, AGN, *Diezmo*, vol. 22, fol. 36.
[2] M. Abad y Queipo, 'Representación a nombre de los labradores y comerciantes de Valladolid de Michoacán... 24 October 1805'; publ. in G. B. Castillo, *Estudios de Abad y Queipo* (Mexico, 1947), p. 36.

2-2

ecclesiastical levy, for more than half of its yield was paid to the civil authorities.

In 1821 the Church had agreed to continue to pay the royal share of the tithes to the new national governments.[1] Three years later, in 1824, it was decreed that the governmental share should be paid to the authorities of the departments in which the tithes were collected. Within a short time the state treasuries began to receive a larger proportion of the revenue than the Church. There were a number of causes of this ironic situation and again the archdiocese provides a good illustration. With the departure to Spain in 1822 of Archbishop Pedro de Fonte the see was considered vacant, and therefore, in accordance with the practice during the colonial period when revenue due to vacant benefices was paid to the monarch, the episcopal share of 25 per cent was paid to the State.[2] The prolonged dispute which arose after independence over the right of patronage resulted in few senior appointments being made in the Church until 1838. Consequently many positions became vacant and the income due to them was also paid to the State. Hence by the year 1833 the civil authorities were in fact receiving $61\frac{1}{2}$ per cent of the tithe revenue.[3]

In view of the precarious financial condition of the nation it was in the interest of any government to support rather than to attack the tithe levy, for the Church was in effect acting as an efficient tax collector on behalf of the State. Nevertheless, neither the fact that they were granting their political opponents a tax concession, nor that they were depriving the nation of much-needed revenue, deterred the liberals from enacting their law. Wider considerations predominated, for apart from economic benefits to agriculture the liberals were well aware that the tithes represented the only constant source of revenue to the higher

[1] These details are taken from *Exposición del Cabildo Metropolitano...*, 24 May 1827, AGN, *Justicia Eclesiástica*, vol. 67, fols. 193 ff.

[2] By the year 1840, the sum of 432,889 pesos due to the metropolitan prelate had been paid to the civil authorities; account dated 14 October 1840, ACM, *Copias de consultas... desde 1 de enero hasta diciembre de 1844*.

[3] There are two tables which illustrate this position: one forms appendix no. 2 of the *Exposición* cited in note 1 above. Another was published by the Minister of Justice in his annual report in 1825. Finally the percentage figure for 1833 was given in *Memoria que un individuo del Cabildo Eclesiástico de la Catedral de México presenta a la posteridad...*, 1834, AGN, PBN, leg. 200, exp. 2.

ranks of the secular clergy. The financial position of the Church greatly deteriorated with the loss of the tithes, and this could not have come at a worse time, for it was not long after 1833 that even the conservative and pro-clerical administrations began to demand substantial cash loans from the Church.

ᴵThis alarming decline in tithe revenue was not ruinous for the Church as a whole, for there were other sources of income. The Church was the largest single owner of real estate in the country. Most of the ecclesiastical corporations owned properties, both rural and urban, which were rented and the revenue obtained used for the daily expenses and maintenance of each institution. The capital assets of the building fund of the metropolitan see consisted to a large extent of houses, and one author states that by the nineteenth century the Cathedral and various bodies associated to it owned one hundred and seven properties worth 1,040,349 pesos.[1] The hospitals and charitable institutions owned a number of houses and, of course, the brotherhoods and colleges had many others. The largest landlords, however, were the regular orders and the greater part of their considerable income resulted from rents.

As early as 1578 the municipal council of Mexico City felt obliged to ask the king to pass legislation which would prevent the regular clergy from acquiring more property in the capital, as they already had possession of the best available. Again in 1664 the council asked the king to forbid the foundation of more convents or monasteries, to limit the number of properties they could own, and to prevent them from acquiring more. The council regretted that almost all the best real estate was already in the hands of the regular orders and warned that if appropriate measures were not taken they would soon own all property in the city. Such appeals as these seem to have had little effect, for although laws forbidding the donation or bequest of property to the Church were issued, no serious attempt was made to implement them. Hence the regular orders and other ecclesiastical corporations were allowed to continue to accumulate real estate. Unfortunately, few reliable

[1] L. Alfaro y Piña, *Relación descriptiva de la fundación de las iglesias y conventos de México* (Mexico, 1863), p. 15.

accounts have been made of the value of property owned by the Church. With reference to the archbishopric, Phipps states that in 1796 clerical income from rented houses in Mexico City totalled 1,060,995 pesos.[1] Capitalized at 5 per cent this gives a total capital value of 21,219,893 pesos. Her source for these figures seems to have been a census made in 1813 for the purpose of allocating a tax on rental income. Some of the documentation used in making the census has survived.[2] This concerns a request made by the viceroy to the convent administrators for details of the rents received during the previous five years, so that an average figure could be decided upon as taxable. The administrators remitted their accounts but only twenty-three of these have been preserved. They show that in 1813 the average annual yield for the institutions involved was 456,629 pesos, which capitalized at 5 per cent amounts to 9,132,580 pesos. It is interesting to note from these accounts, which give the rental income of each institution for the years 1807-11 that they show virtually no decline in the return in spite of the fact that the war of independence had begun; some even show an increase. Evidently the effects of the war were not yet making themselves felt. It is impossible to estimate with any degree of certainty the total value of property owned by the clergy because to do this every college, brotherhood, and parish would have to be taken into account, in addition to the regular orders and such institutions as the Cathedral. Furthermore, real estate values were in a state of fluctuation after 1821, and in general reflected the changing political situation. For example, in the comparatively stable year of 1839, a clerical official reported that prices were rising. During the American war of 1846-8, however, houses sold in the capital rarely reached two-thirds of their valuation price. Such fluctuations make it almost impossible to give an accurate estimate of the value of Church property. The figures given above, which refer only to the capital city, serve to show that the Church was indeed a substantial owner of property.

[1] H. Phipps, 'Some aspects of the agrarian question in Mexico', *Univ. of Texas Bulletin*, no. 2515 (Austin, 1925), pp. 59-60.
[2] These documents are in AGN, *Conventos y Templos*, vol. XI.

To the liberals such a concentration of property in the hands of totally unproductive corporations like the convents and monasteries was uneconomic, and particularly anomalous in view of the fiscal position of the nation. These opinions were to some extent justified, for a large part of the income of the regular orders was consumed in the daily maintenance of the clergy themselves, who contributed nothing to the material, and apparently very little to the spiritual progress of the nation.[1] The Church maintained that it had as much right to acquire real estate as any private citizen, and furthermore, that its use of its property was of immediate benefit to the community. The houses owned by the ecclesiastical corporations were let to tenants at an annual rent which was generally equivalent to 5 per cent of the capital value of the premises. The administrator of the convent or brotherhood was responsible for selecting the tenants, collecting the rents, and supervising maintenance and repairs. The terms of the tenancy agreements were lenient and the Church would appear to have been a good landlord.[2] There is no evidence to suggest that it abused its extensive ownership of property by price discrimination or the imposition of high rental values. The clergy frequently claimed that it was a positive advantage to have the Church as landlord. Archbishop Lázaro de la Garza y Ballesteros emphasized that individual citizens occupied Church houses and not the clergy themselves, and that the consideration afforded to tenants by the ecclesiastical corporations was far superior to that of private landlords. He himself had often given tenants extra time to pay, or even reduced their rents when they were in financial difficulties.[3] Certainly, the annual accounts of the convent administrators reveal that many tenants were able to avoid paying their rent for long periods, and that the convents rarely received more than

[1] There were many critics of the moral and religious character of the regular orders, and certainly not without justification if the activities of one monk, named Tomás Liz, were typical. A fellow monk reported that Fr. Tomás was continually drunk and *no se ocupa en otras cosas que en frecuentar las tabernas, pulquerías y figones, acompañado de la gente más arrastrada y despreciable para vomitar de su infernal boca blasfemias y desverguenzas...*; undated letter in AGN, PBN, leg. 92, exp. 40.

[2] An example of a tenancy agreement is in AGN, PBN, leg. 1274, exp. 9.

[3] Representation to the Minister of Justice, 1 July 1856; published in F. H. Vera, *Legislación eclesiástica mexicana* (Amecameca, 1887), vol. III, p. 207.

half of the income that was due to them. This, however, was more due to the inefficiency of the administrators than to the charity or benevolence of the corporations.

Clerical revenue from rents was in fact decreasing in the nineteenth century because of a number of circumstances apart from the liberal attempts to confiscate Church property. The political situation restricted the economic growth of the country, with the result that tenants were less able and even more reluctant to pay rents to their ecclesiastical landlords. Certain convents suffered from the government's frequent inability to pay its employees, for the latter were excused payment of rent as long as their salaries were not paid. In addition, government loans forced many of the regular orders to sell houses in order to raise the required capital, and this in turn reduced rental income. Many of the properties were so old that even the considerable amounts which were yearly spent on repairs and renovations were not sufficient to maintain them in a satisfactory condition. Finally, it is clear that administrative ability and organization were lacking in the financial affairs of the regular orders, and few administrators were able to fulfil efficiently their duties.

The situation as regards rented property was obviously conducive to change and encouraged the convents and other corporations to adopt a new fiscal policy of selling real estate in favour of investing their capital. The need to sell was only acute in those corporations which were less well endowed and which had little or no surplus income after all expenses had been met. In such cases the loss of a small amount of revenue would incur a deficit at the end of the year and probably compel the sale of a house. Some convents, notably La Concepción and La Encarnación in the capital, were richer and able to amass considerable sums from income which was surplus to their requirements. The latter were often able to meet government loans without disposing of any of their capital assets. Also, each institution only received a part of the revenue which it was owed each year because of the reluctance of tenants to pay their debts. Hence in years of relative stability the income of some convents increased. The following figures showing the annual income of four convents are taken from accounts made for the personal use of higher members of the Church and are therefore assumed to be reliable:

|  | 1812 | 1833 | 1853 |
|---|---|---|---|
| Concepción | 69,483 | 70,331 | 77,500 pesos |
| Encarnación | 58,748 | 61,496 | 70,000 pesos |
| Regina Celi | 39,036 | 39,513 | 32,000 pesos |
| Sta. Brígida | 7,684 | 16,652 | 13,500 pesos |

It is interesting to note that three corporations increased their revenue in spite of the unfavourable conditions which prevailed in the first half of the century. Even the decrease in the other convent was only slight. The figures given above include the total revenue received from rents and investments but serve to show that although rents were difficult to collect and many loans were made to the government, the overall effects on clerical wealth were not important. The process of acquiring wealth by legacy and donation was continuous and it is probable that the losses suffered by the regular orders were offset by new inheritances. The total annual income of the fifteen convents in the capital city and under the jurisdiction of the prelate confirm this fact:

| 1835 | 457,666 pesos |
|---|---|
| 1847 | 491,395 pesos |
| 1853 | 483,500 pesos[1] |

The above figures represent the nominal amounts of convent revenue. The real value of their income and that of the Church as a whole must have been affected by the changing value of the peso. It is extremely difficult to estimate the changes in the purchasing power of the currency after independence. There are, however, various indications that the cost of staple foods and services did increase and that institutions with fixed incomes such as the religious corporations found difficulty in meeting their rising costs, in spite of the fact that there may have been a slight increase in the nominal amount of their revenues. Individual

[1] These totals have been compiled from three accounts drawn up by the diocesan advisers and accountants. They are respectively in: AGN, PBN, leg. 307, exp. 11 (account entitled *Estado que comprehende las rentas cobradas por los conventos de Sras. Religiosas de esta Capital...*); leg. 81, exp. 1 (document entitled *Memoria secreta, estado num. 6*); leg. 1524, exp. 129 (account entitled *Estado que manifiesta los derechos de glosa...*).

priests with fixed incomes derived from benefices often complained of the rising cost of living and the fact that what had been an adequate stipend in the colonial period was no longer sufficient. Hence it seems probable that the wealth of the Church, in addition to confiscations and forced loans, did suffer from inflation in the currency.

Nevertheless, in spite of liberal hostility and conservative demands for financial help, the regular orders were able to maintain at least the nominal total of their riches throughout the turbulent period following independence. From the liberal viewpoint, their arguments in favour of nationalization of clerical property were equally valid and applicable in 1856 as they had been in 1833, and consequently much of the reform legislation enacted by the Juárez administration was directed against the convents and the monasteries. Yet neither the tithes nor the property owned by the Church had a great effect on the economy, and alone did not justify liberal attacks on clerical wealth, especially as the tithes were virtually abolished after 1833. The liberal attitude was much more influenced by the third and final major fiscal activity of the Church, that is the investment of capital.

Within half a century of the foundation of the Church the clergy had formulated a definite fiscal policy which entailed the investment in real estate of all funds proceeding from benefices, pious works, and monetary bequests. Chevalier has indicated some of the methods of investment which were adopted. For example, landowners who wished to make a pious gift or bequest to the Church sometimes were unable to raise the capital in cash, and therefore they would place a perpetual lien on one of their properties. Chevalier writes:

The lien usually represented the income, at 5 per cent, on a principal that was not paid the beneficiary, nor could it be claimed by him; but the principal was in his name. Many parents made these arrangements for their daughters entering convents; a dowry of 3000 to 4000 pesos, for instance, represented an annual income of 150 to 200 pesos taken from the revenues of a rural estate or rental property. The convent, in a manner of speaking, owned stock in the undertaking.[1]

[1] F. Chevalier, *Land and Society in Colonial Mexico* (California, 1963), p. 253.

The secular clergy in particular used this method for making their capital productive. Funds proceeding from *capellanías* and pious works were used as liens and were invested in every kind of real estate. As many thousands of benefices were founded in the colonial period the situation soon arose in which virtually every hacienda in the country was responsible for a lien and was paying part of its profits to a priest or an ecclesiastical corporation. In the words of Chevalier, 'the real masters of the soil had turned out to be the mortgage holders, that is primarily the Church'.[1]

With the inflow of funds continuous and increasing, the Church gradually evolved a similar but more complicated and significant method of investment. By the eighteenth century the ecclesiastical corporations were investing their funds by giving loans at interest to any person who required them, provided that the borrower could furnish an adequate security. Any person could request the loan of a sum of money for a term of five to nine years during which he would pay 5 per cent interest on the debt, and at the end of which he in theory was obliged to redeem the capital. In practice an extension at the end of the first term was almost always given. There was no restriction placed on the borrower as to the use which he made of the money, and the size of the loan depended entirely on the amount of funds which were available at the time. The most important feature of this system concerned the security which had to be provided before any loan could be considered. In most cases the only acceptable security was real estate. Hence almost all borrowers were property owners and they used their house or farm as a guarantee for the amount they borrowed from the Church.

This lending system had two highly significant results. First, the Church as creditor gained complete control of the security, for the terms of the contract demanded that the tenure of the property mortgaged could not be altered in any way without prior permission of the creditor. Secondly, most landowners found themselves in need of loans, and as they could easily be acquired they did not hesitate to seek them and thereby mortgage their estates. The fact that they were not forced to redeem the loan meant

[1] *Ibid.* p. 257.

that the debt was handed down from generation to generation, and each successive owner found himself having to pay interest to the Church.

Because of the abundance of funds and the constant demand for loans, the Church at the beginning of the independence period had control of a substantial part of all urban and rural property. The personal political implications of this situation can only be supposed, but it would seem a reasonable assumption that a man wanting to borrow or already owing money to the Church and hoping to be granted an extension on his debt, would be unlikely to attack or condemn publicly the fiscal activities of the clergy. Most landowners in this respect had little alternative but to support the clergy, or at least remain silent, in any controversy involving the Church. Furthermore, it is of interest to note that the small businessman or merchant, from whom liberals might expect to gain support, was frequently seeking loans from the Church. On the other hand, the fact that many people were in debt to the ecclesiastical corporations could imply that they would tacitly aid such measures as the abolition of the convents in the hope that their debt would also disappear.

From all points of view, therefore, the political and economic implications of clerical control of real estate were of the greatest importance in the nineteenth century. The Church itself was well aware of this fact and it made strenuous efforts to defend its investments and its fiscal policy against the attacks of the liberals and other economic reformers. At the centre of the controversy was an organization which to date has been almost entirely neglected by historians, and yet which was probably the most influential ecclesiastical institution in the country. This was the *Juzgado de Testamentos, Capellanías y Obras Pías*, which in each diocese was directly involved in and responsible for almost all the investment of clerical wealth. By the end of the eighteenth century the *Juzgado* in the archdiocese had developed into a large commercial enterprise, with many highly skilled employees who were daily engaged in the management and investment of sums totalling several millions of pesos.

The *Juzgado*'s importance as a banking institution cannot be overemphasized. To the aspiring merchant or impecunious land-owner there was no other source from which funds could be borrowed on easy terms. The *Juzgado* in effect exercised a mono-poly in the availability of investment capital. This grave deficiency in the economic structure of the country, which above all required capital investment, was realized by successive govern-ments, both liberal and conservative, and attempts were made to establish alternative banking institutions. The most significant of these was the *Banco de Avío* established by law on 16 October 1830.[1] The aim of this was to provide the facilities for the growth and development of small industry and manufacturing plants. In the words of the law it was to provide the purchase and distribu-tion of machinery needed to stimulate the various branches of industry, and to furnish the capital needed by the companies that were formed or by individuals who devoted themselves to industry. Machines were to be given at cost price and the capital was to carry a 5 per cent interest, the term of the loan being fixed.[2] The idea and eventual foundation of this bank were largely due to the efforts of the powerful conservative politician, Lucas Alamán, but within a few years it had collapsed and been abolished. The reason for its failure illustrates the importance of the *Juzgado*. Chávez Orozco has correctly pointed out that Alamán did not appreciate that the only easily realizable capital in the nation was in the hands of the clergy.[3] Private citizens, who did have substantial amounts of cash, preferred to use their capital in high interest loans to the Public Treasury. Alamán, therefore, tried to attract capital to the bank when in fact there was none to be had. Hence the bank failed and the Church through the *Juzgado* remained the only institution in the country able to provide capital for investment purposes.[4] The following chapters describe the organization and activities of the *Juzgado* and indicate the way in which clerical capital was employed.

[1] The foundation and development of this bank have been studied in R. A. Potash, *El Banco de Avío de México. El fomento de la industria, 1821–1846* (Mexico, 1959).
[2] Dublán y Lozano, vol. II, pp. 293–4.
[3] Cited in E. L. López, *El crédito en México* (Mexico, 1945), pp. 136–7.
[4] The Church viewed its lending operations as an investment of capital. The actual term used was *imposición de capitales a réditos*.

# CHAPTER I

# THE 'JUZGADO DE CAPELLANIAS'. ORGANIZATION AND EMPLOYEES

Each diocese had its own *Juzgado*, which was generally located in the episcopal palace.[1] The one in the archbishopric occupied several rooms on the ground floor and in the year 1838 its director, Dr D. Felipe Osores, wrote to the chapter to complain of the lack of space and the need of an additional room.[2] He explained the inconveniences of the present accommodation and pointed out the obvious dangers of keeping the money chests in the same room to which the public were daily admitted for the conduct of their business. He emphasized that because most of the coinage received was in copper, four large chests at least were needed, and these filled every spare corner at one end of the room. The other end was used to receive and count the money and there was hardly space for the table. Hence because the public seemed to see nothing but overflowing money ches tsthere was a general misconception about the wealth of the *Juzgado*. He then recalled that only recently thieves had attempted to open the doors with skeleton keys, probably encouraged by the mistaken belief that the chests contained great amounts. Moreover, the attempt had been made in broad daylight between seven and eight in the morning, and according to the only porter in the building the thieves had had the effrontery to return to measure the locks on the doors. New ones had since been installed but these could easily be forced open and the solitary porter was powerless to prevent such robberies. The office in which records were kept was also cramped and in confusion. Money was counted there but as it was again mostly in copper, the employees were engaged the whole morning. The noise made by the latter disturbed the Chief Notary whose desk was nearby, and not only inconvenienced the

---

[1] Juan Manuel Irisarri to Minister of Justice, 17 October 1848, AGN, *Justicia Eclesiástica*, vol. 154, fol. 166.

[2] Dr D. Felipe Osores to Chapter, 1 March 1838, AGN, PBN, leg. 1172, exp. 50.

officials but also any public business, for there was no space for chairs for the lawyers and litigants. Auctions had to be held almost at the door of the *Juzgado* and when there was a large number of people present, some had to remain outside.

All these problems, concluded Dr Osores, could be eliminated by the addition of an empty room at the side of the present offices. The money chests could be moved into this and any expenses incurred in its conversion would be borne by the funds of the *Juzgado*. Unfortunately, the document from which this information is taken gives no indication as to the result of the request.

The risk of robbery had been considered some years earlier. in 1815, when the chief treasurer of the diocese wrote to the director, then Dr D. Pedro Flores Alatorre, to inquire whether the money kept in the chests was sufficiently well guarded.[1] The director replied that the doors to the offices were each locked with a different key, that the windows also locked and were protected by iron bars, and finally that a military barracks situated nearby provided a further safeguard. He was of the opinion that the money was perfectly safe and pointed out that the employment of guards would add to costs.[2]

The confidence in his security arrangements expressed by the director turned out to be unjustified, for some two years later the *Juzgado* was broken into and robbed. On 5 November 1817 José Mariano Díaz de Guzmán, a minor official, arrived at the office at 9.15 in the morning to find that the main doors were already open. Inside he found that the money chests had been forced open and also the drawer in the Chief Notary's desk. The thieves had used candles to see and several keys were found scattered on the floor. The robbery took place at a time when the offices were closed for four days during a public holiday and 2,490 pesos were stolen. The director wrote that the theft had been committed by someone who had concealed himself and slept within the episcopal palace. There was evidence against the soldiers who were supposed to guard the building, for they were

---

[1] Dr D. Miguel Casimiro to Judge, 25 April 1815, AGN, PBN, leg. 709, exp. 11.
[2] Judge to Dr Casimiro, 29 April 1815, *ibid.*

well acquainted with the daily routine of the *Juzgado* and had
often seen how and where the money was kept.[1] Again the
document from which this information was taken does not
indicate whether the thieves were ever apprehended.

The *Juzgado*, therefore, occupied several offices and its employees were numerous. Some worked on a full-time basis and
others only part-time. Changes in the numbers and types of posts
within the organization, and in particular in the nomenclature
of the various positions, were frequently made, although the
higher administrative ones remained the same throughout the
colonial and independence periods. In the nineteenth century
the full-time employees were generally as follows:

> Judge (*Juez*)
> Fiscal Adviser (*Defensor Fiscal*)
> Chief Notary (*Notario Mayor*)
> Chief Assistant Notary (*Notario Oficial Mayor*)
> Assistant Notary (*Notario Oficial 2°*)
> Archivist (*Archivero*)
> Legal Adviser (*Defensor Abogado*)
> Agent (*Agente 1°*)
> Agent (*Agente 2°*)
> Scribe (*Escribiente*)
> Idem
> Idem
> Treasurer (*Tesorero*)
> Accountant (*Oficial de cuenta y razón*)
> Money Counter (*Contador de moneda*)
> Notary Treasurer (*Notario Receptor*)
> Idem
> Idem[2]

The director and head of the *Juzgado* was known as the 'Judge
Ordinary, Inspector of Wills, *Capellanías*, and Pious Works'
(*Juez Ordinario, Visitador de Testamentos, Capellanías y Obras Pías*).
This appointment was made by the head of the diocese and the

[1] Dr Alatorre to Sr D. Juan de Apodaca, 5 November 1817, AGN, PBN, leg. 538, exp. 34.
[2] This list of employees is dated 5 December 1859, AGN, PBN, leg. 355, exp. 19. For
other lists see AGN, PBN, leg. 960, exp. 11, and AGN, *Justicia Eclesiástica*, vol. 47,
fol. 103.

person selected was invariably a member of the chapter. The following persons held this important position during the first half of the nineteenth century:

| | |
|---|---|
| –1803 | Dr D. José María Bucheli |
| 1804–1809 | Dr D. Juan Francisco Taxava |
| 1810–1814 | Dr D. Pedro de Fonte |
| 1815–1823 | Dr D. Félix Flores Alatorre |
| 1824–1830 | Dr D. Ciro de Villa y Urrutia |
| 1830–1834 | Sr Lic. Joaquín José Ladrón de Guevara |
| 1835–1852 | Dr D. Felipe Osores |
| 1852– | Dr D. Salvador Zedillo[1] |

The director was responsible to the Archbishop or the governing chapter and almost all his decisions had to be approved by one or the other of these higher authorities. His decrees regarding the investment of capital, which was his main responsibility, had to be approved by four members of the chapter known as the Associate Judges (*Jueces Adjuntos*), and in any doubtful case, or one which involved an exceptionally large sum, the advice and consent of the prelate was sought.

On 1 February 1825 the chapter wrote to the Judge, Dr Ciro de Villa y Urrutia, to complain that loans had recently been given without the knowledge and assent of the Associate Judges.[2] All loan negotiations were to be suspended until the matter had been settled. Dr Urrutia defended the prerogatives and rights of his position and claimed that it had never been the custom in the three hundred years existence of the institution to inform the Associate Judges of loan extensions or judicial cases. The only person to be informed in such circumstances was the Legal Adviser who represented the diocese. Moreover, it had never been the practice to inform the chapter of the imposition of funds proceeding from newly established benefices.[3] The reply of the chapter indirectly rebuked the Judge by recommending to his attention the decrees of 30 January 1728 and 30 January 1747, by which any money invested by the *Juzgado* had to be approved by the Associate

[1] This list has been compiled from the records of the *Juzgado*.
[2] Chapter to Judge, 1 February 1825, AGN, PBN, leg. 429, exp. 65.
[3] Judge to chapter, 7 February 1825, *ibid*.

Judges. The latter laws were to be obeyed and the same principle was to apply to extensions of loan contracts.[1]

The activities of the Judge were, therefore, closely supervised, although at least in one sphere his decision was independent of any higher authority. This involved the patronage of certain benefices and pious works exercised by the head of the *Juzgado*.[2] His work mainly consisted of giving his approval to proposed loans before sending them to the Associate Judges, of supervising the foundation of *capellanías* and pious works, and of appointing *capellanes*, although again such appointments had to be approved by the ruling prelate or chapter. The real importance and influence of his position lay in the fact that he was able to refuse any request made to him, whether it be for a loan or for appointment to a benefice, without reference to his superiors. Therefore, to the prospective borrower or aspiring *capellán*, the director of the *Juzgado* was the person of importance.

Much of the power inherent in the Judge's position had disappeared by the beginning of the nineteenth century. In the colonial period he had acted, as his title implies, as Inspector of Wills, and had adjudicated in all disputes over bequests in which the Church had a claim. Phipps states that this power was abused and cites as evidence the laws passed in an effort to restrict clerical intervention in testamentary cases.[3] One of such laws was issued on 27 April 1784, and a copy was sent to the Archbishop by Sr D. Vicente de Herrera y Rivera, Regent of the Royal *Audiencia*, who asked that the Judge be informed.[4] On 8 October 1784 the prelate ordered that a copy of the decree should be sent to the *Juzgado* and that it should be obeyed.[5] Hence clerical control over one of the most important sources of revenue to the Church was virtually removed, and in the nineteenth century almost all cases involving wills and legacies were heard in the civil courts.

[1] Chapter to Judge, 21 February 1825, *ibid*. I have been unable to locate these decrees. There is no mention of them in the minutes of the meetings of the chapter. For this information I am indebted to P. José Espinosa Gutiérrez, who examined the minutes on my behalf.

[2] For a list of these, see AGN, PBN, leg. 734, exp. unmarked.

[3] Phipps, p. 50.

[4] V. de Herrera y Rivera to Archbishop, 28 September 1784, AGN, PBN, leg. 266, exp. 58.

[5] Decree of Archbishop, 8 October 1784, *ibid*.

Within the *Juzgado* all employees were responsible to the Judge, who, although not having the power to dismiss, could suspend an employee and recommend to the prelate that he be dismissed. The two employees next in seniority to the director were the financial and legal advisers, known respectively as the *Defensor Fiscal* and the *Defensor Abogado*. The former was appointed by the head of the see and was responsible for advising the Judge on any financial matter in which the *Juzgado* was involved. For example, when a request for a loan was received it was the duty of the Fiscal to consider the proposals regarding interest, the term of the loan, and above all the security offered as mortgage. When a guarantor was required he was expected to know the financial and character reliability of each person proposed; he had to check the valuations of property which were submitted, and he had to recommend the terms under which the contract should be drawn up. The Judge always accepted the advice of his adviser concerning any proposed loan. The Fiscal was probably the most industrious of all the employees, for his reports on loan negotiations were almost always several pages in length and filled with details on property valuations and calculations regarding the suggested security.[1] Apart from having a very extensive knowledge of both civil and canon law he had also to be an accomplished judge of character, for the decision in fact rested with him as to whether a person would fulfil his obligations and pay the interest on any money that he might borrow from the *Juzgado*.

The Legal Adviser was of similar importance and it was his duty to advise the Judge on judicial matters pertaining to testamentary cases in which the *Juzgado* was a beneficiary, or to bankruptcy cases in which it was a creditor. Any court action to be taken against borrowers was handled by him and he had to present monthly a list of all cases in which the institution was involved, indicating the progress made in each one, and the date when each was undertaken.[2] The amount of business carried out by his office, known as the *Defensoría*, would seem to have been

[1] Such industry was only shown in the nineteenth century, for the advisers in earlier periods rarely produced more than a few lines.
[2] *Reglamento Provisional de la Defensoría de Abogado*, 20 June 1843, AGN, PBN, leg. 1283 exp. 1.

considerable and attempts were made to relieve the burden of the work imposed on him. On 26 January 1843 the Archbishop issued a decree which began by stating that the number of cases which the Legal Adviser had to deal with was so great that in spite of his proven efficiency and constant and exclusive dedication to his work, he was physically incapable of completing them or even pursuing them, with the result that many were paralysed and irreparable damage was being caused to the pious works concerned.[1] A few months later, two additional assistants were appointed to work in the legal office at a salary of four hundred pesos a year.

The remaining employees were of considerably less importance. The Chief Notary was in effect secretary to the Judge and all the decrees of the latter were issued through him. In 1789 a new post was established entitled the Notary of Masses (*Notario de Misas*). This was the result of advice from the Fiscal who pointed out to the Archbishop a number of deficiencies in the administrative system then operated.[2] He wrote that most *capellanías* contained a clause according to which the beneficiary had to say, or to arrange and pay for a number of masses to be said for the soul of the founder. Unfortunately, there was no employee specifically charged with ensuring that such terms of the benefices were in fact fulfilled, and consequently in many cases the masses were not said. Furthermore, *capellanías* were often awarded to persons who at the time were not ordained members of the Church. Such persons always promised to be ordained as soon as possible but there was no way of knowing if they ever were. Hence people with no vocation or inclination towards the priesthood were enjoying the income from benefices even though they had perhaps joined the army or been married. In order to avoid this kind of evasion the Fiscal suggested the appointment of a new employee whose main duty would be to keep a record of the following facts: every appointment of a *capellán* who had not been ordained, details of the benefice and its founder, the number of masses stipulated in the terms of each foundation, and finally, the

---

[1] Decree of Archbishop, 26 January 1843, AGN, PBN, leg. 1693, exp. 4.
[2] Fiscal Adviser to Archbishop, 9 January 1789, AGN, PBN, leg. 575, exp. 47.

age of the *capellán* which had to be taken directly from the baptismal certificate. The first person appointed to this post was in fact the then Chief Notary, Mariano Becerra.[1] In the various lists of employees which were made in the nineteenth century there is no further reference to the Notary of Masses, and therefore it seems likely that the post was in fact combined with that of the Chief Notary.

The secondary notaries were mainly employed in minor tasks such as reading to interested parties the decrees of the Judge and the Advisers, and informing prospective borrowers of the results of their applications for loans. Consequently, much of their time was spent in going around the city in search of *capellanes*, debtors, and hopeful borrowers. They were not Public Notaries and hence were not authorized to attest loan contracts which were enforced under civil law. The Notary Treasurer, as the title implies, was responsible for issuing receipts for money paid into the *Juzgado*.

In 1852 the Supreme Court of Justice informed the prelate that the notaries employed in the *Juzgado* should all be laymen. The Archbishop consulted his advisers, who in a report dated 20 March 1852 declared that regardless of the present ruling made by the Supreme Court the Chief Notary had often in the past been an ecclesiastic.[2] In fact, it is clear from the records of the *Juzgado* that most of the notaries were laymen. The position of Chief Notary was held from at least 1824 to 1859 by Lic. Atilano Sánchez, who was included in a list of employees entitled 'secular individuals'.[3]

The function of employees such as the treasurer, the archivist, and the scribes requires no explanation. The Business Agent had the unpleasant task of taking possession of property or goods which had been adjudicated to the *Juzgado* in legal cases, and he was also responsible for collecting interest from borrowers who had refused to pay the collector. It is interesting to note that until

[1] Decree of Archbishop, 14 January 1789, *ibid.* The need for the new employee continued for many years: see *Lista de los Capellanes cuyas capellanías tienen calidad, y no consta haberse cumplido, así como los que teniendo 25 años de edad, no se han ordenado, según informa la Notaría de Misas.* August 1856, AGN, PBN, leg. 230, exp. unmarked.
[2] *Vicario Capitular* to Archbishop, 20 March 1852, AGN, PBN, leg. 717, exp. 14.
[3] List of employees dated 18 September 1824, AGN, PBN, leg. 960, exp. 11.

the year 1843 an interpreter of Indian languages was employed, who enjoyed a salary of 200 pesos a year.[1] The need for this employee is not immediately apparent, for it is unlikely that the Indian population was in a position to borrow money from the *Juzgado*, mainly because in most cases real estate was demanded as security for any loan and few Indians were property owners.[2] However, ecclesiastical records do reveal a possible function of the interpreter. Among the many wills in these records there are a number written in a native language.[3] It is probable that the richer chiefs and Indians made bequests to the Church and in such cases the services of an interpreter might be required. The position was abolished in the year 1843.[4]

The above-mentioned employees worked in or near the offices of the *Juzgado*. In addition to these there were various other part-time staff and advisers. Administrators were often appointed to manage the finances and property of those pious works which had been particularly well endowed, and as the *Juzgado* served all parts of the archbishopric, the limits of which extended into five states, authority was often delegated, usually to local priests to represent the interests of the Church in the more remote parts of the see.[5] In 1833 the Judge appointed a special collector to be responsible for the interest on those funds which had been invested outside the limits of the diocese.[6]

However, the majority of the *Juzgado*'s interests and activities were centred on the capital city, and a Property Administrator (*Administrador de Fincas*) was employed to manage the interests in property. Although the institution did not in theory own any real estate, in practice about forty houses were administered by its officials during the early part of the nineteenth century. These

[1] *Reglamento Provisional...*, AGN, PBN, leg. 1283, exp. 1.
[2] In the colonial period loans were often given without real estate as security but instead several guarantors of recognized wealth were required.
[3] For example, *Testamentos de indios del pueblo de Mixcoac, traducidos al castellano*, 1665, AGN, PBN, leg. 414, exp. 37.
[4] The possible reasons for this are interesting: it may indicate a declining influence of the Church among the Indians with a subsequent drop in legacies, or perhaps a decline in the numbers speaking only a native language. In either case the need for an interpreter would decrease.
[5] For example, see AGN, PBN, leg. 27, exp. 45; leg. 591, exp. 6.
[6] Decree of Judge, 28 January 1833, AGN, PBN, leg. 1172, exp. 15.

properties usually formed part of the principal fund of a benefice or pious work but some had been ceded in payment of debt.[1] At the beginning of the century the administrator, D. Juan Nepomuceno Vasconcelos, had to provide two sureties, each of two thousand pesos, but by the year 1834 the number of houses to be managed had so decreased that the Fiscal advised that one surety was sufficient.[2] The person appointed to the post signed a contract in which his duties were outlined. The money collected must be paid into the coffers monthly, and general accounts were to be presented annually detailing all items of income and expenditure; the administrator was not allowed to concede tenants time in which to pay without the express permission of the Judge, and if he defaulted on one monthly payment into the *Juzgado* he would be automatically suspended; any legal matters were to be referred to the legal adviser, and finally he was responsible for the repairs and general maintenance of the properties, which meant that he must inspect them regularly.[3]

The administrator was not under constant supervision and therefore the temptation to defraud the *Juzgado* must have been present. Every effort was made to appoint an honest and efficient person but in the nineteenth century at least the selection methods seem to have met with little success. The most frequent complaint against the administrators was their refusal or inability to submit the accounts of their activities. For example, in 1817, after several previous orders, the then administrator, Sr Vasconcelos, was given three days in which to present his accounts.[4] In 1846 Francisco Herrera y Campo was ordered to do likewise but replied that he was too busy to do so because of his other commitments as a deputy in the General Congress.[5] It was not until some fourteen years later, after many threats had been issued, that Herrera finally remitted his accounts on 6 January 1860.[6]

---

[1] For details on these properties, see chapter 2.
[2] Dr Cabeza de Baca to Judge, 31 May 1834, AGN, PBN, leg. 967, exp. 23.
[3] Decree of Judge, 8 July 1833, AGN, PBN, leg. 967, exp. 23.
[4] Decree of Judge, 4 July 1817, AGN, PBN, leg. 538, exp. unmarked.
[5] F. Herrera y Campos to Notary Ignacio Cureño, 12 January 1847, AGN, PBN, leg. 284, exp. 23.
[6] F. Herrera y Campos to Judge, 6 January 1860, *ibid.*

This lack of control over its staff indicates a certain inefficiency in the organization, and other examples are not difficult to find. On 5 July 1833 the Judge wrote to the chapter, then governing the diocese, to ask its assistance in a matter pertaining to the administrator, Pres. D. Juan Araujo.[1] He had been appointed on 21 May 1827.[2] Since that time he had not presented any accounts in spite of the threat of legal action being taken against him. Moreover, in compliance with the terms of his contract he had offered a house as security, which he had claimed to own. Investigations had now revealed that the officials responsible for his appointment had not checked his surety, and furthermore had neglected to ensure that Araujo had signed his contract, which, it now appeared, he had not done. As he was ill and unable to carry out his duties, the Judge wished to appoint a temporary collector to do so. He also asked that the administrator should be required to submit a surety and if he failed to do so, that he should be immediately suspended from office. The following day the chapter authorized the appointment of a temporary collector until Araujo had regained his health and presented all outstanding accounts. The Judge proceeded to name Joaquín Cadena and outlined his duties. Cadena presented his sureties, which were accepted, and he was confirmed in the appointment. As Cadena continued to present accounts for several subsequent years it can be assumed that he was eventually appointed as administrator. There is no evidence to indicate that Araujo ever did submit the details of his administration.[3]

The funds which were entrusted to the care of the *Juzgado* in the form of benefices or pious works were normally invested at interest to yield a certain income. The interest was collected by an employee generally known as the Collector or Administrator of Rents (*Recaudador o Administrador de sus rentas*). In fact he collected income from several sources, referred to in the accounts as: pious works, embargoes, estates, coffers, *capellanías*, borrowers.

[1] Judge to chapter, 5 July 1833, AGN, PBN, leg. 967, exp. 23. Araujo was the only cleric to occupy the position of property administrator in the nineteenth century.

[2] Chapter to Judge, 21 May 1827, AGN, PBN, leg. 265, exp. 9.

[3] For some accounts of the various administrators, see AGN, PBN, leg. 361, exp. 3; 958/3, 780/1, 793/12, 800/3.

However, from the year 1825 *capellanes* were allowed to collect the interest from their own benefices.[1]

Another employee in the same category as the above was the Collector of Rents of Vacant Benefices (*Recaudador de Vacantes*). If a *capellanía* or any benefice became vacant it was his responsibility to collect the income of the foundation and to ensure that those who had borrowed the principal fund continued to pay interest on the loan. His duties were similar to those of the other collector and the appointments were sometimes combined. The money collected was to be paid into the *Juzgado* daily and if on occasion this proved impossible it must be paid in at the end of the week. The Judge could ask for accounts at any time and such losses as were found in these were to be made up by the collector. Automatic suspension would result from a failure to comply with any clause in the contract within two months.[2] In the year 1846 the two positions of Collector of Rents of Vacant Benefices and Property Administrator were combined in the appointment of Mariano Malda, the Archbishop having previously given his consent to the joint appointment.[3]

The payment of employees was based on the general principle that those of professional status received only fees for their services, whereas the remainder were paid a salary. One particular exception to this was the Legal Adviser, who enjoyed both fees and salary. The remuneration of those employed in collecting was approximately five per cent of the amount collected. The scale of fees used in the nineteenth century was that issued on 3 June 1789 by Archbishop Alonso Núñez de Haro y Peralta and in 1852 Archbishop Lázaro de la Garza y Ballesteros sent a copy of this tariff to the Minister of Justice informing him that it was still in use.[4] The following are some of the amounts charged. For the

---

[1] A detailed search in the records of the National Archive and the Cathedral Archive did not reveal the exact date of this change in the system of collection. However, the Chief Notary sent letters to borrowers informing them of the change and some of these have survived, for example, Atilano Sánchez to Sra. María de Jesús Ariscorreta, 7 April 1825, AGN, PBN, leg. 27, exp. 91.

[2] Decree of Judge, 29 March 1843, AGN, PBN, leg. 1178, exp. 2.

[3] The documents concerning this appointment are in AGN, PBN, leg. 582, exp. 13.

[4] Archbishop to Minister of Justice, 8 January 1852, AGN, *Justicia Eclesiástica*, vol. 169, fol. 73.

decree ordering the investment of any capital of a benefice or pious work, which was to be given with only guarantors, the Judge's fee was eight pesos, that of the Public Notary four pesos, and that of the Chief Notary two pesos and four reales. If a mortgage of property was involved the fees rose accordingly, being twelve, five, and four respectively. The regulations emphasize that these sums represent the maximum that was to be charged, and that they were not to be increased in any way. For the decree declaring a capital redeemed the fee was seven pesos, four to the Judge and three equally divided between the Public Notary and the Chief Notary. The Fiscal received two pesos four reales as a fixed rate for most of his work, for example, for deciding on the patron of a benefice or who should be named *capellán*. In those matters which required an exceptional amount of work it was left to his conscience to charge a just amount.[1]

It is to the credit of the Judges and the various officials that there appears to have been few complaints of overcharging during the nineteenth century.[2]

Complaints were made of bribery. In 1849 the state legislature of Mexico presented a report in which it was stated that the Congress was already acquainted with the abuses committed by almost all the administrators of clerical goods.[3] For example, in loan transactions the borrowers were obliged to sign a contract for a greater amount than they actually received. Sometimes the interest rate was raised to 6 per cent and it was well known that the borrower had to agree to pay all present and future taxes levied in connection with the transaction. Finally, it was alleged that bribes of considerable amounts had to be paid in order to be granted a loan or to have the term of an existing one extended. It is impossible to prove or disprove these allegations, but perhaps

[1] This table of fees is in AGN, *Justicia Eclesiástica*, vol. 169, fols. 94–103. There is another copy in AGN, PBN, leg. 1537, exp. 15. Both are printed documents. Receipts for payment of services rendered by the *Juzgado* are to be found in AGN, PBN, leg. 173, exp. 1.

[2] One exception to this is in AGN, *Justicia Eclesiástica*, vol. 180, fols. 14–31.

[3] *Exposición que la legislatura del estado libre y soberano de México eleva a la Cámara de Diputados sobre el decreto sobre redención de capitales piadosos* (Toluca, 1849).

it is significant that similar charges were made at the end of the eighteenth century.[1]

The salary of the lesser employees was paid monthly. The amounts in 1845 were as follows:

### Notaría Mayor

| | |
|---|---|
| Chief Notary, two scribes and archivist | 166. 5. 4. |
| Reviser of accounts | 50. |

### Tesorería

| | |
|---|---|
| Treasurer Administrator | 83. 2. 8. |
| Official | 50. |
| Money Counter | 25. |

### Defensoría

| | |
|---|---|
| Legal Adviser | 83. 2. 8. |
| Agent | 33. 2. 8. |
| Agent | 33. 2. 8.[2] |

In addition to these employees there were several minor notaries and proctors who received no salary and who were probably only called upon in times of exceptional activity, when they would receive a fee for their work. In the year 1811 an interesting custom was established. These minor officials wrote to the chapter to complain of their poverty and to request that a gift be given to each of them. The chapter ordered that the matter be referred to the Judge and that if money was available it should be given.[3] Eventually the employees were granted various amounts which depended on their individual needs, bachelors receiving fifty pesos and married men with large families one hundred pesos.[4] More than thirty years later, in 1845, the officials wrote to the Judge saying that the time had again arrived when the director

---

[1] With reference to obtaining a loan from the Church one writer states: '...pues, además de las fianzas regulares para el seguro del principal y réditos, tienen que exhibir casi una tercera parte de la cantidad por razón de propinas, obsequios y gratificaciones;' Enfermedades políticas que padece la capital de esta Nueva España en casi todos los cuerpos de que se compone; y remedios que se le deben aplicar para su curación si se quiere que sea útil al público (20 May 1785), p. 8: published in Voz de la Patria, suplemento no. 1, 11 September 1830.

[2] These details on salaries are taken from a book of accounts which covers the whole of the year 1845. Payments were made at the end of each month. The book is in AGN, PBN, leg. 1026, exp. 3.

[3] Decree of chapter, 20 December 1811, AGN, PBN, leg. 437, exp. 5.

[4] Undated account, ibid.

showed his generosity towards them by awarding a gift for their many days of service throughout the year.[1] They pointed out they received no fixed salary and could not live on what they made in fees. The time was again December, which meant that in effect they were asking for the Christmas present which it had become customary for the *Juzgado* to give. On this occasion the employees, who numbered ten, were given only twelve pesos each, a much smaller sum than that which their predecessors had received.

It is evident that the *Juzgado* was a relatively large and complex organization, and although an ecclesiastical institution the majority of its staff were not ordained members of the Church. In spite of its apparently business-like administration it was sometimes criticized on the gounds of inefficiency. In 1850 the office hours were from 9 a.m. to 1.30 p.m.[2] A few years later, in 1856, Archbishop Lázaro de la Garza y Ballesteros complained in a letter to the Judge that the *Juzgado* was inefficient.[3] The prelate maintained that the protracted length of the negotiations with the institution had become notorious in the city and he blamed this on the fact that the hours during which the offices were open to the public were not sufficient, and that the employees began too late in the morning and finished too early in the afternoon. He ordered that the *Juzgado* should remain open to the public for at least five or six hours daily. On receipt of this letter from the prelate the Judge issued a decree to be read to all employees by one of the notaries. In future the office hours were to be 8.30 a.m. to 2 p.m. The notaries were to attend from 11 a.m. to 1 p.m. The Chief Assistant Notary then proceeded to inform all the employees of the latter decree and most had indignant comments to make about the criticism directed at them by the Archbishop. The second notary, José María Aparicio, probably felt that it applied to him in particular, for he was in charge of the keys and

---

[1] Employees to Judge, undated, 1845, AGN, PBN, leg. 1026, exp. 3.
[2] *Vicario Capitular* to Minister of Justice, 20 June 1850, AGN, *Justicia Eclesiástica*, vol. 166, fol. 228. These times were ordered to be published by the Minister and they appeared in the *Periódico Oficial del Supremo Gobierno de los Estados Unidos Mexicanos*, Saturday, 22 June 1850.
[3] Archbishop to Judge, 8 March 1856, AGN, PBN, leg. 472, exp. 11.

was responsible for opening the doors each morning which, he
maintained, he did punctually at 9 a.m. in accordance with a
previous decree of the Judge. Other employees claimed that they
had always worked the four hours prescribed by the director and
added that their emoluments were so small that they had to have
time to pursue other occupations. Without exception all denied
having been late.

Such charges of inefficiency against the organization of the
*Juzgado* were rare, and by and large its relations with the general
public, which occupied most of the officials' attention, would
seem to have been good. Nevertheless, from the viewpoint of the
Church the internal operation of the institution does not seem to
have been entirely satisfactory, for very large sums of money were
lost to the apparent unconcern of the Judge and his advisers. Very
few changes in personnel and methods were made in the nineteenth century in spite of the vastly different circumstances in
which the Church found itself, and, although there was a decrease
in the activities undertaken and the jurisdiction of the Judge had
been restricted, it appears that the size and extent of the business
was still too great for the institution to manage effectively. The
*Juzgado* in fact suffered a gradual decline throughout the first four
decades of independence which ended in its eventual disintegra-
tion as a result of the reform laws enacted by Juárez in 1861. It was
in January of this year that government officials ransacked the
offices and removed all the papers and records that they could
find to the National Palace where they remain today.

CHAPTER 2

# THE 'JUZGADO' AND ITS REVENUE

The activities and business undertaken and conducted by the employees described in the previous chapter involved and were dependent upon the revenue of the *Juzgado*, which resulted mainly from the three sources mentioned in the title of the institution, namely wills, *capellanías*, and pious works. To some extent these three sources overlap, for benefices and pious works were usually established by will. Indeed, income from legacies was throughout the colonial period a most important branch of ecclesiastical finance and bequests of enormous amounts were made.[1] It seems probable that almost every person who was financially able to do so did leave some form of legacy to a clerical corporation. The administration of the majority of these donations was entrusted to the *Juzgado*.

The most common form of bequests were the *capellanía* and the pious work. The latter requires little comment. Many people left funds or property, the income from which was to be devoted to a pious work. For example, in the year 1796 Juan Acosta left 200,000 pesos to the Church and this sum was to be invested to yield an annual income of 8,000 pesos.[2] Half of the income was to be devoted each year to the establishment of a *capellanía*, and the other half was to be used for the dowry of a novice wishing to take the final vows. Most of the charitable institutions managed by the clergy were supported by monetary gifts and legacies, and money was often left towards the maintenance of an orphanage or hospital. The benefactor would have the required deeds drawn up,

[1] One magnificent bequest was made in 1651 by Alvaro Lorenzana who, having already built the church of La Encarnación at his own expense, left the Church 800,000 pesos in cash, houses, and furniture, 20,000 pesos for masses and prayers for his own soul, 20,000 pesos to the convent of La Merced, a small legacy for every nun in Mexico City, and various gifts to the Jesuits; cited in A. Toro, *La Iglesia y el Estado en México* (Mexico, 1927), p. 33.

[2] Documents concerning this bequest are in AGN, PBN, leg. 1412, exp. 7. By 1830 the capital had already decreased by half; see decree of Judge, 8 May 1830, AGN, PBN, leg. 1412, exp. 14.

stating the proposed terms and conditions of the foundation, and would then ask that it be accepted by the Church.[1] If all was found to be in order the trusteeship of the pious work was usually given to the *Juzgado*, which was responsible for the administration and distribution of the income from the principal fund. In certain cases, particularly where a large sum of money was involved, the prelate would appoint a special administrator, who was required to present his accounts directly to the diocesan accountant, and not to the officials of the *Juzgado*.

The most important source of revenue, however, came from *capellanías*, and the procedure involved in the foundation of these benefices was detailed and complicated. The terms were generally stated in the form of clauses in a will, although occasionally the legator would merely instruct his executors to use a proportion of his goods for the formation of a *capellanía*, and he would leave the details of beneficiaries and conditions to the trustees of his estate. In most cases, detailed instructions were stipulated. The founder would instruct his executor to establish a *capellanía* with a certain sum, usually between 2,000 and 6,000 pesos, the income from which was to be given to the recipient of the benefice who was known as the *capellán*. The latter, in return for this income, would be obliged to say annually a certain number of masses for the soul of his benefactor. If the named recipient had not been ordained, or was not yet of age to enter the Church, he was expected to pay another priest to say the masses until he himself was qualified to do so. Even after being ordained, the *capellán* could pay another priest to carry out the terms of the benefice. The clauses in the deeds of each foundation invariably contain a long and comprehensive list of alternative and future recipients, and these were normally the direct and indirect descendants of the founder.

A patron was also named who was given the right to designate the *capellanes*, and the future patrons were stipulated in the same way as the future recipients. The right of patronage was of importance because in later generations the patron was often able to appoint himself as *capellán*, when the line of *capellanes* originally stated in the foundation had died out. The executor would

---

[1] An example of such a deed is in AGN, PBN, leg. 1760, exp. 1.

present the deed of foundation and ask the Judge to admit the proposed foundation into the Church, to accept the *capellán*, and to make the goods 'spiritual and ecclesiastic'. The Judge would seek the advice of the Fiscal and if he reported all to be in order he would accept the foundation.

The following account of an actual *capellanía* will illustrate the above procedure in more specific detail.[1] In 1665 Doña Teresa de Caballero Padilla, a woman of considerable wealth and property, died in Mexico City. In her will she instructed her sister, Doña María, to arrange the foundation of a *capellanía* with a capital sum of 2,000 pesos, to yield an income of 100 pesos per annum. She named her sister as patron, which gave her the right to decide on the appointment of the *capellán* who was to enjoy the fruits of the benefice. The duties of the latter were to say a mass for Doña Teresa's soul every Monday in the convent of Santa Inés. Her sister, Doña María, began to arrange the *capellanía* and had drawn up the appropriate deeds. Her own children and relatives were named as future patrons in a certain order of preference. The first *capellán* was to be Bachiller Bartolomé Rosales, 'a cleric in minor orders, a person virtuous and poor'. He was the proprietary *capellán* and as such was to receive the income from the benefice. As he was still in minor orders he was not permitted to say the masses himself and, therefore, he was instructed to appoint a priest to do so and to pay him an adequate amount. The latter priest was known as the acting *capellán*. The deeds were then submitted to the *Juzgado* and read before the Judge. The Fiscal, to whom the matter was referred, recommended acceptance. A few years later, when Rosales became a full member of the Church he was confirmed in the benefice and the goods pertaining to it were again made 'spiritual and ecclesiastic', which meant that they could not be 'sold, ceded, exchanged, nor in any way alienated without the express permission of the Judge of the *Juzgado*'.

This *capellanía*, originally established in 1665, remained under the control of the Church until 1798, when it became vacant through the death of the then *capellán*. No new claimants for it could be found and hence the Fiscal advised the Judge that in

---

[1] The records of this benefice are in AGN, *Capellanías*, vol. 1, exp. 3.

accordance with a royal decree of 4 February 1798, the patronage of the foundation devolved upon the Crown, and that all the documents concerning it should be forwarded to the Viceroy. On receiving these, the Viceroy handed them over to the Temporalities Office which began to reorganize the benefice. Eventually it was rearranged as a purely lay foundation and given to an academically good but financially poor student of theology in the College of San Ildefonso.[1]

By accepting a *capellanía* into the Church the *Juzgado* undertook to administer and organize all matters pertaining to the benefice in the future. This involved a dual responsibility, for on the one hand it had to ensure that the ecclesiastical laws concerning it were observed, and on the other hand that the monetary value was carefully safeguarded. For example, with regard to canon law, no person under the age of fourteen could be the holder of a *capellanía*, but sometimes this rule was relaxed. In 1839 Joaquín Núñez de Ribera wrote to the head of the archbishopric to inform him that his brother Manuel had been named *capellán* by the patron of a benefice established by Bernardo de Tapia.[2] Unfortunately, his brother was only eight years of age and hence under normal circumstances could not be allowed to accept the foundation. Ribera pointed out that his brother was an orphan with very few resources and he asked that the age limit should be reduced in this case. The *Vicario Capitular* replied that evidence must be supplied to verify these facts, and as soon as he was satisfied as to the genuine need of the young boy he decreed that age rule need not be applied.

Flexibility in the interpretation and application of canon law inevitably resulted in differences of opinion, but the *Vicario Capitular* was correct in the above case. This is proved by a dispute which arose in the Puebla diocese between the bishop of the see and Miguel de Echevarría, who at the age of fifteen had claimed the income from two *capellanías*.[3] He was the proprietary *capellán*

---

[1] The *capellanía* was still in existence in 1841; AGN, *Justicia Eclesiástica*, vol. 110, fol. 150.
[2] J. Nuño de Ribera to *Vicario Capitular*, undated, 1839, AGN, PBN, leg. 761, exp. 16.
[3] These details are taken from a printed pamphlet found in the British Museum. See *Mexican Political Pamphlets*, no. 3, B. M. catalogue no. 9770, k. 2. (3).

of these but because he was under age the prelate had appointed an interim *capellán* and had ordered that the latter should receive all the income. The case was eventually taken to Rome for settlement, where it was pleaded before a committee of cardinals charged with interpreting the laws issued by the Council of Trent. The following questions and answers were resolved by this court. Was it necessary to be of age to receive an ecclesiastical benefice? The cardinals decided that it was necessary to be of age to obtain a *capellanía* on a permanent and complete basis within the Church, but that those not of age could hold the benefice under the title of *Administrationis*. The next question asked whether the right to appoint an interim *capellán* belonged to the bishop of the diocese or to the patrons of the benefice, and it was decided that this right belonged to the patrons, in spite of the fact that it had been the custom of the bishop of Puebla to make such appointments. Finally, it was declared that the income from a *capellanía* should be paid to the proprietary *capellán*, who in the case in dispute was the plaintiff.

The main work of the *Juzgado*, however, was not so much concerned with questions of canon law as with the practical administration of each benefice. Hence when both the *capellán* and the patron had died, the Judge would announce the vacancy and invite candidates to come forward to claim the foundation or the patronage of it. An announcement was placed on the doors of the Cathedral and if the founder had been long resident in another part of the diocese one was also placed on the doors of the parish church in the town in which he had lived. The following is an example of the announcement:

To those persons concerned with the contents of this edict I make known: that Presbyter D. Felipe Patiño established an ecclesiastical *capellanía* with a principal of 3,000 pesos, to which he designated as patrons and proprietary *capellanes*, after some named persons, the sons, grandsons, and descendants of D. José Patiño de las Casas and Doña María Quirós, the eldest being given preference over the youngest, and the nearest to the most distant relative, and as patrons the male descendants in preference to the female. The patronage and possession of this benefice were obtained by D. Francisco Patiño, Treasurer and Dignitary

of this Holy Church, and with his death they are now vacant. Therefore, I summon each and every person who may have a right to either
the patronage or possession, that within a maximum of thirty days
of the publication of this edict, they should appear in this *Juzgado*
personally or through an attorney, to make their claim formally. When
the stipulated period has ended I will proceed to the appointment of the
patron and proprietary *capellán* as appropriate. Issued in the *Juzgado de
Testamentos, Capellanías y Obras Pías* of this archbishopric and stamped
with the seal of the Archbishop on 31 January 1852.[1]

At the end of thirty days the Judge and the Fiscal would
examine the claims and decide which had the greatest right to the
benefice. Sometimes all the claimants were of equal merit,
particularly in those cases in which the benefactor had merely
ordered that the *capellanía* should go to a poor but worthy student.
Such foundations invariably attracted a host of applicants and
there was no alternative but to choose the *capellán* by lot.[2] Having
selected the new recipient the Judge would then issue a decree
summarizing the main clauses in the terms of the benefice and
ending with a standard declaration, of which the following is an
example:

...his Worship said: that he determined and declared as proprietary
*capellán* of the said *capellanía* the aforementioned Presbyter Bachelor
D. Manuel Salarza, for the duration of his life, who as such, fulfilling
the obligations of the benefice, will receive the income as from today,
and who must present himself within the next two months before the
governing chapter in order that he may be given collation.[3]

The responsibility of the Judge did not end here. Many
thousands of *capellanías* were established during the colonial
period and most of the officials were concerned with the daily
organization of these benefices.[4] The principal of the foundation
was invested by the *Juzgado* and the interest was collected by its
employees. This system was frequently criticized by the *capellanes*

[1] Decree of Dr D. Salvador Zedillo, 31 January 1852, AGN, PBN, leg. 27, exp. 66.
[2] For example, in 1836 there were dozens of applicants from several towns for a *capellanía*
arising from the foundation established by Juan Acosta. The eventual recipient was
chosen by lot; AGN, PBN, leg. 1412, exp. 14.
[3] Decree of Lic. J. J. Ladrón de Guevara, 28 April 1831, AGN, PBN, leg. 82, exp. 66.
[4] The records of many of these *capellanías* are in AGN, *Capellanías*.

who felt that they should be allowed to collect the interest on their own benefices. In 1822 José Leonardo Castrellón, representing two *capellanes*, complained to the Judge that the houses in which the *capellanías* of his clients had been invested were being allowed to fall into disrepair.[1] He maintained that the properties were becoming more and more dilapidated and if urgent repairs were not immediately carried out they would soon be worthless. Because of their poor condition, the rental value was very low with the result that his clients were receiving less than one third of the interest that was due to them. They now wanted him to administer the properties and he asked permission to do so. This the Judge granted on 5 November 1822. There are many similar examples in the records of the *Juzgado* and it is not surprising that in 1825 the Judge decided to allow any *capellán* to collect the interest on his own benefice if he wished to do so.

Sometimes efficiency within the *Juzgado* seems to have been lacking. In 1827 Santiago Aranguren, representing the *capellán* Dr D. Vicente Simón González de Cosío, wrote to the Judge to complain that the interest due to his client was not being received.[2] He alleged that more than four months previously he had personally gone to the *Juzgado* to collect the money due from the benefice. He had received nothing on that occasion, and since then no payments had been made, with the result that his client had suffered considerable hardship. He appealed to the Judge to order that the long overdue interest should be paid and that an account of the finances of the foundation should be drawn up. The Judge ordered that the interest be handed over immediately but whether this was done remains unknown.

The number of benefices administered was so great that some confusion and inefficiency were inevitable, particularly when one remembers that the records of many of the foundations dated back more than two centuries. Nevertheless, some faults were often not caused by bad administrative machinery but by poor organization, or even idleness on the part of the employees. On 31 December 1846 Manuel José Araoz, chief collector, submitted

[1] J. L. Castrellón to Judge, undated, 1822, AGN, PBN, leg. 1106, exp. 7.
[2] S. Aranguren to Judge, undated, 1827, AGN, PBN, leg. 27, exp. 80.

his accounts for the years 1845 and 1846. These were sent to the
chief accountant who presented his report on them on 13 December
1847.[1] He observed that the amount gathered was not even a
quarter of what it should have been. He commented that the
collection made by Sr Araoz had been very poor and that the
results of his efforts seemed to confirm what his own office had
constantly maintained, that is, that almost all of the *Juzgado*'s
capital was paralysed or even lost. Time alone would prove or
disprove this but he could only hope that he was mistaken in his
criticism.

The *Juzgado* certainly did lose a great deal of its capital through
inefficiency. The major problem confronting the clerical officials
was that they were unable to maintain a constant supervision over
each *capellanía*. Consequently, unknown to the Judge, numerous
benefices became vacant and the persons who were in possession
of the principal fund of the foundation ceased to pay the interest
because nobody came to collect it. This created problems for both
the holder of the capital and any new *capellán* who was appointed
to the benefice. In 1825 Cándido Lajaraso wrote to the Judge as
follows.[2] He was the owner of a farm in the district of Toluca in
which the principal fund of a *capellanía* amounting to 4,000 pesos
had been invested at 5 per cent annual interest. He had always
paid the interest punctually, but on 20 April 1822 the *capellán* had
died. Since that time he had not paid any interest because nobody
had come to collect it. He therefore owed 600 pesos and the
*Juzgado* had now demanded that he must pay this sum immediately.
He maintained that he was unable to pay such a sum all at once
and he appealed for time in which to raise the money. He pointed
out that throughout the difficult years of the war of independence,
when his farm had suffered considerable loss from damage and
theft, he had always made sure of paying the *capellán*. He was
unable to find the amount demanded because in recent years
the produce of the farm had scarcely covered the costs of production and had left him with no surplus capital. He ended by asking
that he be allowed to pay off the debt at the rate of 100 pesos

[1] J. Irisarri to Judge, 13 December 1847, AGN, PBN, leg. 1209, exp. 6.
[2] C. Lajaraso to Judge, undated, 1825, AGN, PBN, leg. 1106, exp. 7.

per year. In his reply the Judge ordered that the debt must be reduced at the rate of 200 pesos yearly, the first payment to be made at the beginning of the next year. As the Judge's letter was dated 17 December he in fact granted the debtor very little time.[1]

In part the *Juzgado* was to blame for the above situation because it was responsible for collecting the interest. The clerical officials, however, would no doubt have maintained that it was also the borrower's duty to pay his debts and that Sr Lajaraso should have made some effort to send the money directly once he knew the *capellán* had died. The *Juzgado* was not reluctant to admit that it often had little idea of the actual state of the finances of many *capellanías*. The Chief Notary, Atilano Sánchez, wrote in December 1826 that there was in the archive a list of the *capellanías* established within the archbishopric but that the list was virtually useless because nobody knew whether the principal fund of each benefice was still active or had been lost.[2]

Some years later, in 1855, the problem was still evident and the Fiscal suggested the introduction of a new system of book-keeping.[3] This was necessary, he argued, because it was the only effective way of avoiding in the future the serious problem which occurred when *capellanías* became vacant without the knowledge of any member of the *Juzgado*. Furthermore, a new method was required of ensuring that the masses prescribed in the terms of each foundation were in fact said. Finally, something had to be done to prevent the loss of the principal funds of the benefices, for as the Fiscal pointed out, not all borrowers had the delicacy of conscience to inform the *Juzgado* when no one came to collect the interest. In spite of the appropriateness of these suggestions, they went unheeded, for in a separate report the Legal Adviser maintained that the book system already in use was adequate. But in reply to an inquiry from the *Archicofradía del Santísimo Sacramento* concerning benefices belonging to the brotherhood the true picture was given. An unnamed official, probably the Chief Notary, wrote that because of the order in which the numerous

[1] Judge to C. Lajaraso, 17 December 1825, *ibid.*
[2] A. Sánchez, unaddressed, 23 December 1826, AGN, *Justicia Eclesiástica*, vol. 96, fol. 166.
[3] Fiscal to Judge, 9 July 1855, AGN, PBN, leg. 284, exp. unmarked.

records of *capellanías* were inventoried it was impossible to discover how many or which belonged to the *Archicofradía*.[1]

In spite of the concern shown by some of the officials over this problem, many benefices were in fact allowed to remain vacant, some for several decades, with the full knowledge of the Judge. On several occasions accounts of these were compiled. One made in the year 1805 indicated that benefices to the capital value of 556,950 pesos were vacant.[2] The income from these was collected and in theory safeguarded until a *capellán* was appointed. The *Juzgado* also arranged for the terms of the foundation to be carried out during the time of the vacancy. The fact that so many benefices were permitted to remain vacant did not go unnoticed by the civil governments, particularly in those times when the financial position of the national exchequer was critical. As early as 1824 a circular was issued to every diocese ordering that an account of all vacant *capellanías*, in which the patronage belonged to the government, should be sent to the Temporalities Office.[3]

In the archbishopric the circular was forwarded by the chapter to the Judge, who eventually replied that only one such benefice was then vacant. At least on this occasion the *Juzgado* does seem to have attempted to answer the governmental inquiry. Twelve years later, in 1836, the Ministry of Justice and Ecclesiastical Affairs made a similar request but the Judge replied that it was impossible to provide the required information.[4] He said that to do so would involve the examination of the records of more than 4,000 benefices and that this task was so enormous that a special investigator would have to be appointed. Again in 1842 the Minister of *Hacienda* wrote to the Archbishop over the question of vacant *capellanías*.[5] On this occasion it was suggested that the Church could help the government with

---

[1] Unsigned to *Archicofradía del Santísimo Sacramento*, undated, 1855, AGN, PBN, leg. 284, exp. unmarked.

[2] *Lista por abecedario de las capellanías vacantes de que ha dado razón el Juzgado de Capellanías*, 20 April 1805, AGN, PBN, leg. 958, exp. 32. For a later account, see leg. 1106, exp. 7: this covers the years 1827–32 and has details of 205 vacant *capellanías*.

[3] AGN, *Justicia Eclesiástica*, vol. 33, fol. 34.

[4] Judge to Secretary of Justice, 28 January 1836, AGN, *Justicia Eclesiástica*, vol. 130, fol. unmarked.

[5] Minister of *Hacienda* to Archbishop, 25 August 1842, AGN, PBN ,leg. 355, exp. 19.

its desperate shortage of money by giving it the interest from the vacant *capellanías*.

A further cause of difficulty in the administration was that the territorial extent of the activities was at times too great. The collectors did not have the time or inclination to travel any considerable distance outside the capital, and consequently in the more remote parts of the diocese much invested capital and interest were lost. In 1835 José Araoz sent an account to the Judge in which he listed the funds which were invested outside the capital.[1] In his words it was difficult to collect the interest on these, and the capital value, apparently given up as lost by Araoz, amounted to 509,563 pesos.

The work of the Judge and his officials not only extended widely in the Republic but also reached indirectly to Spain. With the war and subsequent declaration of independence a number of *capellanes* returned to the peninsula. This posed an unusual problem, for there was no reason why a person should be deprived of his benefice because of his residence in another country. Before leaving, the *capellanes* had taken the precaution of appointing representatives to collect the interest of their benefices and it was to these that the *Juzgado* paid the revenue until 1824. Then in August of that year the Minister of Justice wrote to the chapter to inquire if the interest was in fact being paid to *capellanes* who were not resident in the country.[2] On being told that the legal representatives were being paid, the Minister ordered that such payments should be stopped until further notice. He then asked for a list of the *capellanes* and representatives involved. This was sent by the *Juzgado* and twenty-three persons were named.[3] On 18 September 1824 the Minister advised the Judge that the interest should still be collected but that the money should be retained for the time being. He now requested details of all the benefices involved, and in particular wanted to know the principal fund of each one.[4] This information was sent to him in October and

---

[1] M. J. Araoz to Judge, 3 April 1835, AGN, PBN, leg. 1139, exp. 10.
[2] Minister of Justice to Governor of the See, 4 August 1824, AGN, *Justicia Eclesiástica* vol. 38, fol. 108.
[3] This list is in AGN, *Justicia Eclesiástica*, vol. 38, fol. 114.
[4] Minister of Justice to Judge, *ibid.* fol. 115.

showed that the total capital value of the foundations was 358,472 pesos.[1]

For the next few years it seemed as if the government was to take no further action in the matter, but then on 10 January 1829 the Minister of *Hacienda* issued a circular letter to the dioceses in which he ordered that all funds in the *Juzgado* belonging to people residing out of the republic should be transferred to the public treasury departments.[2] He was forced into this demand, he said, because of the constant poverty of the government. On 12 January the Judge informed the secretary in the Ministry of Justice that he had ordered the sum of 6,000 pesos to be paid immediately into the General Treasury Office. He claimed that this was the amount left after the cost of paying for the masses stipulated in the terms of each foundation had been met, and after the collector's 5 per cent had been deducted.[3] Within a few days the Minister of *Hacienda* wrote to his colleague in the Justice Department to say that there should have been much more than the 6,000 pesos that had been handed over. This comment was passed on to the Judge, who replied that although the total in interest payments may have been about 11,000 to 12,000 pesos, only 6,000 remained after all the costs had been met. However, after only three days he again wrote to the Secretary of Justice to inform him that a further 1,888 pesos was being handed over to the Treasury.

Two more years passed and then on 2 June 1832 the Minister of Justice again ordered that the interest accumulated since 1829 should be handed over to the government.[4] This order was referred to the *Juzgado* by the chapter and after several further demands from the government the Judge wrote to say that although the accounts had not yet been liquidated he was sending the sum of 2,000 pesos on account.[5] Eventually on 30 July the Judge informed the Minister that all the accounts had now been

---

[1] Judge to Minister of Justice, *ibid.* fol. 130.
[2] Circular of Minister of *Hacienda*, 10 January 1829, *ibid.* fol. 13.
[3] Judge to Secretary of Justice, 12 January 1829, *ibid.* fol. 16.
[4] Minister of Justice to chapter, *ibid.* fol. 67. Another letter repeating the same order and dated 30 June 1832 is in AGN, PBN, leg. 743, exp. 4.
[5] Judge to Secretary of Justice, 2 July 1832, *ibid.* fol. 86.

examined and that the total liquid sum in interest collected from the vacant benefices was in fact less than the 2,000 pesos which had already been given. He enclosed the details to prove this and expressed the hope that the government would return some of the money.[1] The accounts show that there were thirty-one *capellanías* held by persons residing abroad and that the total interest on these between the years 1824 and 1832 amounted to 11,891 pesos. From this had to be deducted 3,987 for the cost of the masses, 1,301 for the collector's fee, 6,000 given to the government in 1829, and several other smaller amounts which had been handed over on different occasions. The final result was that the *Juzgado* had paid the government 1,055 pesos too much. It is doubtful whether this was ever repaid.

The following year, 1833, the government again ordered the *Juzgado* to pass on the money that had been collected,[2] and it was clear that the Church was in effect being used as a collector on behalf of the State. This situation continued until 1838 when a commercial treaty was signed with Spain. The latter was dated 28 February 1838 and within less than one month the Judge wrote to the Minister of the Interior to say that because of article three of the treaty a number of people had come to claim the interest on the vacant *capellanías* held by persons outside the Republic.[3] He asked whether he should pay them, and if so, that the previous order of 1824, whereby the *Juzgado* was told to retain the interest, should be revoked. The matter was referred to a governmental committee and on 2 May 1838 Lucas Alamán, a member of the committee, wrote that under the terms of the peace treaty the money should be paid to the legal representatives of the *capellanes*. This decision was communicated to the Judge on 8 May.[4]

The importance and value of the *capellanía* suffered a considerable decline in the nineteenth century. This type of benefice was designed to provide a fixed income sufficient to maintain a priest and to enable him to pray for the soul of his benefactor. Hence

---

[1] Judge to Minister of Justice, 30 July 1832, *ibid.* fols. 89–91.
[2] Minister of Justice to Judge, 5 September 1833, *ibid.* fol. 92.
[3] Judge to Minister of Interior, 22 March 1838, AGN, *Justicia Eclesiástica*, vol. 110, fol. 175.
[4] Minister of Interior to Judge, 8 May 1838, *ibid.* fol. 180.

the amount of the principal fund was determined by the annual income which it would yield. In the early colonial period an income of between 100 and 150 pesos a year was sufficient to maintain a priest and hence the capital of each *capellanía* was usually between 2,000 and 3,000 pesos, which, when invested at 5 per cent simple interest, would produce the required yield. By the nineteenth century, however, living costs had risen to such an extent that an income of this amount was no longer adequate, particularly if the *capellán* had to pay another priest to say the masses. In 1820 one writer claimed that the income from a *capellanía* was no longer enough even for food.[1] The problem was in fact recognized by the Crown at the beginning of the century. A royal decree of 4 August 1801, directed specifically to the bishopric of Oaxaca but intended for general circulation, accepted the view of *capellanes* that the terms imposed by many of the founders of benefices were excessive, in particular with regard to the number of masses to be said.[2] The decree recommended that the masses should be reduced but it was left to the prelates to decide the appropriate number for each foundation.

After independence the problem was still evident. In 1832 Basilio Arrillaga wrote to the dean and chapter to ask that the number of masses he had to say should be reduced.[3] He was the beneficiary of three *capellanías* which yielded the sum of 411 pesos per year. His duties were to say or have said one hundred and sixty-seven masses each year and he maintained that this number was excessive in view of the small yield of the benefices. He pointed out that the cost of food, houses, and salaries, presumably referring to the fees payable to priests who said the masses, had all risen. Another interesting point he made was that the great scarcity of priests in the archdiocese meant that it was often very difficult to find anyone prepared to say the mass. Because of this

[1] *Representación dirigida al Ilmo. Señor Arzobispo de México* (Mexico, 1820).
[2] A copy of this decree is in AGN, PBN, leg. 115, exp. 14.
[3] B. Arrillaga to chapter, 6 June 1832, AGN, PBN. leg. 1172, exp. 12. A person of the same name was some years later to attack Dr Mora's opinions on clerical wealth. If it was this *capellán*, he clearly had a vested interest in defending Church goods: see, B. Arrillaga, *Cartas por B. Arrillaga al Dr. Mora citándole a responder por los fundamentos y resultados de sus opiniones sobre bienes eclesiásticos, producidas en el tomo primero de sus obras sueltas* (Mexico, 1839).

shortage the minimum fee now charged was one peso. Finally the masses could only be said in the church of the convent of Balvanera and this restriction was causing him difficulty. He asked, therefore, that he be allowed to arrange them in other churches and that the annual number should be reduced. Both these requests were granted.

A further problem confronting many of the *capellanes* in the nineteenth century concerned the capital value of their foundations. Often part of the principal fund was lost, either through the bankruptcy of the person with whom it had been invested, or through the inefficiency of the *Juzgado* which allowed the benefice to remain vacant. In such cases the amount of interest was reduced, sometimes to a negligible amount, and the benefice was practically useless. In 1831 the Minister of Justice noticed what was happening and he suggested that when the principal fund of a vacant *capellanía* had greatly diminished in value, the interest payments, however small, should be capitalized each year, thereby creating a new and more substantial sum.[1] Once the original amount of the benefice had been reached, a new *capellán* could be appointed and ordained. The Minister asked if there was anything in canon law which might prohibit this procedure. His proposals were forwarded to the *Juzgado* and the Fiscal reported that the idea seemed sensible and that to his knowledge there was nothing in canon law to prevent it being implemented.[2]

It is clear, therefore, that the value and function of the *Juzgado* depended to a large extent on the *capellanía*. Almost all of its activities were in some way related to this specific kind of benefice, and to the Church as a whole its value was incalculable. The clerical attitude to these foundations was explained by the Fiscal in 1813.[3] He wrote that the *capellanías* were not completely clerical benefices, but rather trust funds which the founders had established for the benefit of members of their family, and hence in the terms of almost every one, preference in the order of recipients was given to close relatives. In spite of their secular nature they were

[1] Secretary of Justice to chapter, 11 January 1831, AGN, *Justicia Eclesiástica*, vol. 103, fol. 262.
[2] Fiscal to Judge, 22 January 1831, AGN, PBN, leg. 556, exp. 10.
[3] Dr Cabeza de Baca to Archbishop, 2 December 1813, AGN, PBN, leg. 330, exp. 29.

virtually the sole patrimony enjoyed by the clergy in America, and it was only through them and the small income which they provided that almost all the ministers of the Church were able to be ordained and maintain themselves. The organization and administration of these benefices was without doubt of the utmost importance to the Church, and the successful financial development of the latter throughout the colonial period must in part be attributed to the work of the *Juzgado*.

However, as I have already indicated, the importance of the *capellanía* began to decline early in the nineteenth century, and this must have been a contributory factor to the shortage of clergy experienced by every diocese in the country. The laws passed in 1798, by which clerical wealth was taxed, perhaps marked the beginning of the decline. Following these were the laws of consolidation, implemented during the years 1805–9, which were specifically directed against *capellanías* and pious works, and many of these foundations were ruined because the principal sum with which they were endowed was confiscated. This fact would probably discourage prospective benefactors from founding new benefices until the political situation had become more stable. This, of course, did not happen and the succeeding years until independence in 1821 must have seen the establishment of few *capellanías*.

After independence a number of reasons combined to reduce even further the number of *capellanías* and as a result the wealth of the *Juzgado*. The political situation did not allow the economic resources of the country to be developed, and few people can have been able to make generous bequests to the Church or to establish benefices for the use of their descendants. Furthermore, the rise of the liberal party and its subsequent struggle with the clerical and conservative groups indicated that the spiritual control which the Church had exercised during the colonial period was decreasing. Finally the general tax laws passed during the nineteenth century caused the bishop of Peubla to declare in a pastoral letter in 1847 that no one with any common sense would think of founding a *capellanía* in the present circumstances.[1] Hence this

[1] *El Católico*, 30 January 1847.

type of benefice ceased to be a permanent and reliable source of revenue to the Church in the sense that comparatively few new foundations were made in the nineteenth century. However, this fact only marginally affected the immediate activities of the *Juzgado*, for the many established during three centuries of colonial rule still had to be administered.

The *Juzgado* enjoyed income from one other source which although minor from the monetary viewpoint was of considerable significance in the general importance of the institution. The main fiscal activity of the Judge and his officials was concerned with the investment of the capital funds of benefices, but partly as a result of this function the *Juzgado* gained possession of a number of properties which in theory belonged to a pious foundation, but which in practice were owned and administered by the Church.

These properties were managed by the Property Administrator and were mostly those which had been embargoed for debt. The accounts of the several administrators employed in the first half of the nineteenth century reveal that the number of houses involved varied between thirty and fifty, and that the approximate average income from these was in the region of 11,000 pesos per annum. Shortly after independence was declared, the officials of the *Juzgado* seem to have decided on a new policy and gradually began to dispose of the houses until by 1837 the number had been reduced to twenty-seven, with a capital value of 118,709 pesos.[1] By the end of the following year this had decreased to twenty.[2] By the year 1846, when the positions of Property Administrator and Collector of Rents of Vacant Benefices were combined in the appointment of Mariano Malda, the real estate owned by the *Juzgado* was reported to consist of a mere seven houses and one rancho, all of which Malda informed the Judge were in need of repair.[3]

The method used to dispose of the properties was to offer them for sale in a public auction held within the offices of the *Juzgado*.

[1] Certificate of tax issued by the *Administración General de Contribuciones Directas*, 8 July 1837, AGN, PBN, leg. 27, exp. 91.
[2] Account of Joaquín Cadena, 11 October 1838, AGN, PBN, leg. 265, exp. 9.
[3] M. Malda to Judge, 29 December 1846, AGN, PBN, leg. 582, exp. 13.

This course of action might be the result of an offer to purchase by a prospective buyer, but it was more usually the result of a decision by the director. In 1829 the architect retained by the *Juzgado* to advise on such matters, indicated that several properties were in very poor condition.[1] The Judge decided to sell them by auction and a few weeks later the following announcement appeared in the press:

In the *Juzgado de Testamentos, Capellanías y Obras Pías* of this archbishopric, three houses are offered for sale, located in the lane of the D. Toribio tavern, and numbered 16, 17, and 18. The three houses have been valued in total at 717 pesos. Any person who wishes to make a bid should go to the aforesaid *Juzgado* where he will be given the necessary instructions.[2]

In July 1842 José Barrera wrote to the Judge to offer to purchase a ruined house at a valuation price fixed by an architect. Realizing that the *Juzgado* would probably only sell by auction he offered to pay the costs of the latter.[3] The Judge ordered that the opinion of the administrator be sought before any action was taken. The latter advised that the property should be sold because it was almost beyond repair. The Judge then ordered that the house should be valued by the architect Joaquín Heredia and advertised for sale. While awaiting the valuation he also decreed that an account should be drawn up of the rental income and any capital which had been invested in the property. The architect estimated the value at 3,650 pesos and the treasurer reported that the rent had amounted in the previous year to 89 pesos and that there were no mortgages.[4] The administrative efficiency of the *Juzgado* then apparently disappeared, for it was almost one year later that Barrera wrote to the Judge urging him to arrange the auction.[5] On 25 September 1843 the latter ordered that the auction should be held on the second day of the following month

[1] José Agustín Paz to Judge, 26 January 1829, AGN, PBN, leg. 366, exp. unmarked.
[2] This announcement appeared in *Correo de la Federación Mexicana*, 26 February 1829, vol. III, no. 270.
[3] J. M. Barrera to Judge, undated, 1842, AGN, PBN, leg. 1505, exp. 4.
[4] These details are taken from correspondence in the above-cited *legajo* and *expediente*.
[5] J. M. Barrera to Judge, undated, 1843, *ibid*.

and that this fact should be advertised. Five days later the advertisement appeared:

The Judge of *Capellanías* of this archbishopric has designated the morning of the second day of October next for the auction of the house known as no. 2 San Antonio Abad street, valued at 3,650 pesos. Any person wishing to bid for this property should present himself in this *Juzgado de Capellanías* where he will be given the appropriate details and instructions regarding procedure.[1]

The auction was held and the house sold to Barrera for 2,550 pesos, which was 1,100 pesos less than the valuation price.

Although there is no doubt that the revenue of the *Juzgado* suffered a considerable decline in the nineteenth century, it is not possible to give an exact figure of the total income and capital due from all sources.[2] This is because the accounts that were made were never complete, and as in the case already cited of Sr Araoz, the sums collected often represented only a small part of the total amount that was due. Furthermore, the modern scholar is faced with the same problems that confronted the Judges in the nineteenth century. They themselves did not know exactly how much of the capital had been lost over the previous centuries, nor which of the invested funds were yielding the correct interest. Also there was the difficulty of the vacant benefices in which the principal fund may have been lost or may not have been returning interest because nobody bothered to collect it.

Again, the *Juzgado*'s income from certain sources, for example legacies, was not a fixed or stable amount and inevitably varied from year to year. General economic and political conditions at times affected the ability of many borrowers to pay the interest on their loans, and particularly during the long war of independence a considerable number seem to have had great difficulty in meeting their financial obligations. In such circumstances revenue declined. However, because of the nature of the fiscal policy, that is investment of capital, an exact numerical figure of the

---

[1] This advertisement was printed in *Diario del Gobierno*, 30 September 1843, vol. XXVII, no. 3021.
[2] Some figures are available of the current active capital of the *Juzgado* at the beginning of the independence period. I have given these in chapter 4.

## The 'Juzgado' and its Revenue

*Juzgado's* revenue is not essential to an appreciation of the importance of the institution and its activities. This is because the *Juzgado* applied the same rules and maintained the same control over its investments regardless of the size of the amounts involved, and its enormous influence resulted from the way in which it used its income.

CHAPTER 3

# PERSONAL LOANS FROM
# THE 'JUZGADO'

The person who established a *capellanía* did so in the hope and
expectation that it would endure perpetually, for the purpose of
the benefice was that the principal would provide an income to
enable a cleric to say a stipulated number of masses each year for
the soul of the founder. Although the *capellán* would die, the
monetary fund providing the income would endure, and, therefore, a succession of *capellanes* would continue in perpetuity to
pray for their benefactor. The pious works were likewise intended to provide a continuous source of income with which to
carry out the desired charity. As the Church was the only institution which could be considered honest, permanent and perpetual,
the trusteeship of these foundations was inevitably given to it,
and within the Church the *Juzgado* was the specific organization
charged with the management of the finances involved. Therefore,
the nature of the revenue which the *Juzgado* received caused it to
act as a type of investment company or bank.

The other ecclesiastical corporations, notably the convents, also
received large sums in the form of legacies and other sources of
revenue, for example, alms and dowries yielded considerable
amounts, particularly in the colonial period. One of the ways
chosen by the convents for utilizing their surplus income and for
safeguarding their future needs was investment at interest.

The method adopted by the *Juzgado* for safely investing the
capital and acquiring the necessary interest on it was to extend
loans at interest to any person who could offer sufficient security
to guarantee the loan. Real estate was considered the only
satisfactory security and therefore all borrowers in the nineteenth
century were property owners. The prospective borrower would
offer his house or farm as security and if he failed to fulfil the
conditions of the loan contract the *Juzgado* as creditor was entitled
to appropriate the property. The amounts loaned were rarely

66

very high—usually being about 4,000 pesos, that is the approximate average value of one *capellanía*—probably because the demand for loans was so great that there was not time to accumulate large sums. The only criteria used to fix the amount of the loan were the value of the security and the ability of the prospective borrower to pay the stipulated interest.

Money was rarely loaned to corporations or institutions except in special circumstances, for example, during the war of independence when many loans were granted to the civil authorities under such securities as the tobacco monopoly revenue and various taxes. That these loans were unusual is indicated by the title of the document on which they are listed which is 'Extraordinary Mortgages'.[1] The reluctance to grant loans to the government authorities probably resulted from the failure of the latter to pay the interest on their debts. After 1821, together with the other ecclesiastical corporations, the *Juzgado* was occasionally asked to contribute to the loans which the Church as a whole made to the various civil governments, but only rarely did it make any independent loans to civil corporations.

Loans of small amounts to individuals was the method of investment used by the *Juzgado*. Applications to borrow money were made almost daily, either in person or by letter, the latter method being more usual, and on condition that the security offered was satisfactory they were normally granted. The time involved was not usually excessive, although when the money was actually given depended on the amount available in the *Juzgado*, and sometimes in the nineteenth century there were occasions on which it had few or no funds to lend or to invest.[2]

The person seeking a loan was not obliged to state the use he intended to make of the money, although many of them did so in their preliminary communications to the Judge. Most claimed that they needed capital to improve production on their farms.[3] Others wanted to repair property.[4] Some even borrowed money

[1] This document is in AGN, PBN, leg. 27, exp. 84.
[2] For example, in answer to a request for a loan in 1824, the Judge instructed, '*Téngase presente cuando haya dinero*', AGN, PBN, leg. 429, exp. unmarked.
[3] F. S. de Escobeda to Judge, 29 May 1810, AGN, PBN, leg. 645, exp. 21.
[4] Doña Marina Tordanes to Judge, undated, 1826, AGN, PBN, leg. 366, exp. 2.

to pay off debts, for example in 1824 Juan Manuel Irisarri, a prebendary in the Cathedral, wrote to the Judge to ask for a loan of 3,000 pesos. He had assumed certain debts on an *hacienda* which he had recently bought and one of the creditors was demanding settlement of the amount owing to him. He intended to use the 3,000 pesos to pay the latter.[1] Some twenty-one years later, Sr Irisarri again used this method to resolve his financial problems. He now owed 5,500 pesos to the Third Order of San Francisco and asked to borrow an equivalent amount to settle the debt.[2] In both cases, as the security he offered was satisfactory, the loans were granted. Various other reasons were given by prospective borrowers. The convent of Balvanera borrowed 4,000 pesos to conclude the urgent rebuilding which was being carried out on the church of the convent.[3] The same corporation in 1837 borrowed 1,500 pesos from the *Juzgado* to enable it to pay its allotted share of a general Church loan to the government.[4]

Only in exceptional cases did the *Juzgado* take a positive interest in the reasons for and possible uses of a loan. One such case occurred in 1829 when the first president of the nation, General Guadalupe Victoria, having retired from office, began to concern himself with the management of his estates. He requested an unusually large loan of 100,000 pesos to be used in improving his thirteen properties in the state of Vera Cruz.[5] In his report on the proposal the Fiscal, Dr Cabeza de Baca, recommended that the request be granted and one of the reasons he gave was the capital requested would be well employed by the intelligent and industrious General whose efficiency and tenacity were well known. Also the loan would benefit agriculture, which was the one branch of the economy to which everybody concerned in the prosperity of the nation should contribute the utmost attention and assistance.[6] The *Juzgado*, therefore, was willing to grant loans of exceptional

[1] J. M. Irisarri to Judge, undated, 1824, AGN, PBN, leg. 429, exp. unmarked.
[2] J. M. Irisarri to Judge, undated, 1845, AGN, PBN, leg. 284, exp. 4.
[3] Joaquín Gómez, administrator, to Judge, 29 May 1827, AGN, PBN, leg. 987, exp. 9.
[4] Convent to Judge, 12 July 1837, AGN, PBN, leg. 1693, exp. 5.
[5] Guadalupe Victoria to chapter, undated, 1829, AGN, PBN, leg. 1693, exp. 5.
[6] Fiscal to Judge, 11 April 1829, *ibid.*

amounts provided the use of the money was justified and beneficial to the country. As it happened, at that time there were no funds available and it was not until two months later that the Judge ordered that almost 16,000 pesos, which had just been redeemed by other borrowers, should be given to General Victoria. The total eventually given was only 16,774 pesos, which proved fortunate, for in later years neither the principal nor the interest was paid and a dispute over this debt continued between the *Juzgado* and Victoria's heirs for a number of years.[1]

The following example of an actual loan negotiation will illustrate most of the main points involved in the procedure. On 13 October 1837 Lucas Alamán wrote to the Judge, Dr Felipe Osores, to ask for a loan of 4,000 pesos. In his preliminary letter he said that he knew the sum of 4,000 pesos was soon to be paid into the *Juzgado* from the pious work founded by Juan Acosta, and he asked that this money should be loaned to him. He offered as security a house which he owned in the capital, the property having been left to him by his now deceased brother, Dr Juan Bautista Arechederreta. The house was not mortgaged in any way and it had been valued at 10,163 pesos. To prove these latter points he enclosed the relevant documents.[2]

Lucas Alamán was well informed as to the requirements of the *Juzgado* and had prepared all the necessary papers in advance.[3] He sent the certificate declaring the house free of any mortgage and a valuation of the property which he was offering as security. Both these documents were essential, the former being obtained from the Mortgage Office, in which all mortgages in the city had to be registered, and the latter being almost certainly an architect's valuation. The first action of the Judge after receiving a letter requesting a loan from someone less well informed than Alamán was to call for the above-mentioned certificates, without which the negotiation would not be considered. In the case of Alamán this was not necessary and following normal procedure the Judge

---

[1] The documents concerning this dispute are in the afore-mentioned legajo and expediente.

[2] Lucas Alamán to Judge, 13 October 1837, AGN, PBN, leg. 538, exp. 10.

[3] Alamán had a number of dealings with the *Juzgado*, sometimes on personal matters, and others as administrator of the Hospital of Jesus; see AGN, PBN, leg. 1083, exp. 84; 1150/50.

ordered that the letter and documents be sent to the Fiscal for consideration. Some days later the latter presented his report in which he indicated that all was in order and that the proposed security was adequate. He recommended that the loan should be given for five years at 5 per cent annual interest, with the special mortgage of the house indicated by Alamán, and also the general mortgage of all the possessions of the latter.[1] On 20 October 1837 the Judge accepted the report and ordered that all the documents relative to the loan be sent to the Associate Judges for their final approval.[2] The latter approved the loan on 7 November. The time involved in the negotiation had been just over two weeks but Alamán did not actually receive the money until almost eighteen months later, presumably because the sum indicated in his preliminary letter was not available. It was on 21 March 1839 that the Judge issued the order that the money be given to Alamán. The final stage in the negotiation was the signing of the contract, which took place before the public notary José Ildefonso Verdiguel on 6 April 1839. The contract was drawn up by the notary and the basic terms were always the same in each case. The following is an abbreviated version of the one signed by Alamán:

Don Lucas Alamán executes and states: that he has received from the *Juzgado de Testamentos, Capellanías y Obras Pías* of this archbishopric, and by the hand of Presbyter Bachelor Don Pedro Fernández, administrator of the pious work founded by Juan Gerardo de Acosta, the sum of 4,000 pesos in silver coin belonging to the principal fund of the aforesaid foundation; which sum has been received to his entire satisfaction without any grounds for claim, in my presence, and for that which grants the most effective receipt corresponding to the *Juzgado*, in the presence of witnesses, to which I testify; and he binds himself to keep the said moneys in his power by way of deposit, for the time of five years beginning and counting from today forward, during which term or longer period which tacitly or expressly may be granted, he will give and will pay, in this city or in the place in which he is asked, the

[1] Fiscal to Judge, 18 October 1837, AGN, PBN, leg. 583, exp. 10.
[2] It was customary at this stage in the negotiation for the Judge to seek the approval of the beneficiary and the administrator of the fund to be used in the loan. For some reason unknown he did not do so in this case.

interest of five per cent per annum, payments being made at intervals of four months, half-yearly, or yearly, the latter being decided by the person who is responsible for collecting the interest, which must be paid in silver coin of this Republic and not in any other type and without any delay; the interest must be paid without ceasing until the principal sum is redeemed which will be at the end of the five years stipulated. The principal sum must be redeemed in one payment, and in the same silver coin, which he received from the coffers of the said *Juzgado*, regardless of the laws which may be decreed by the civil authority on the coinage in which such payment should be made; the latter being applicable to both the capital and the interest, neither of which should be handed over to any other person on pain of second payment. If by tacit or express consent of the aforementioned *Juzgado* and interested party, the said 4,000 pesos should remain in the possession of the executor of this deed without being redeemed for more than the five years stated, in addition to not ceasing to pay the interest, neither he, his heirs or successors, are entitled to plead limitation, lapse of term, novation of contract, nor any other exception which is directed towards the obstruction or surrender of the executory force of this deed, which in every event and time must be recognized as binding, valid and subsistent, even though a decade or more may pass; cancellation by payment must be in accordance with the relevant legal requirements, and the costs of redemption must be paid by the borrower, and also those judicial or extrajudicial costs which may arise whenever legal action is required to oblige the borrower to fulfil all or part of the contents of this deed. It is an express condition that if any delay is observed in the punctual payment of the interests on the principal, which are stipulated in this deed, even though it may only be a single four-monthly payment, the term of the deposit will be considered ended, and the creditor may seek executively the return of the said capital, and extra payment for the amount owed. And for the greater security of the said 4,000 pesos, and the interests, (the borrower) mortgages expressly and especially, without derogating the general hypothecation of his goods, for the *Juzgado* and interested party may choose one or the other, the house located in the road named Buenavista, on the Rivera of San Cosme, marked with the number eighteen, of which he is the owner. The mortgage includes everything which belongs to the said house, and also additions, repairs and improvements, and the house must not be sold, ceded, given, changed, pledged, nor in any manner disposed of, until the 4,000 pesos have been redeemed and the interests paid. Should the latter condition be broken, this contract will be null and void, and the representative of the *Juzgado* and afore-mentioned pious work may take possession of the house from all future owners, may take judicial or extrajudicial action to effect its sale or foreclosure, and with the resultant product make a complete pay-ment of the total owed in capital, interests, and costs which may be incurred. It is also agreed that the said house bears no other mortgage, which fact is recorded in the certificate of the Municipality; the original of the latter is shown to me so that it may be added to my register, and that a copy may be given together with the copies of this deed. And he (the borrower) accepts obligation to register this instru-ment in the registers of contracts and mortgages of this Municipality within the time prescribed by law, and having fulfilled this requirement, to return it together with the appropriate certificate to the *Juzgado de Capellanías*, so that it might be placed in the archive of the latter. And finally, the executor solemnly affirms that he will fulfil everything contained in this deed as is herein expressed verbo and verbum. And to the punctual observance and fulfilment of everything herein stated, he pledges his possessions, present and future, and he submits himself and them to the laws and jurisdiction of the Judges and justice of this Republic. And in the presence of Dr D. José María Aguirre, Fiscal Adviser to the said *Juzgado de Capellanías*, having read and understood the import of this deed, he said that he accepted it in all its parts. And thus they executed and signed it, the witnesses being D. Ignacio Cureño, D. Francisco Oscoy, and D. Vicente Calderón. — José María Aguirre. — Lucas Alamán. — José Ildefonso Verdiguel.[1]

The contract was signed by Alamán, the Fiscal, and the Public Notary.

The term of the loan was for five years and in March 1844 Alamán wrote to the Judge indicating that he wished to sell to Juan Guijosa the house which he had used as security for the above loan.[2] The latter wished to assume the debt, thus having less to pay in cash to Alamán. In the joint letter, Alamán and Guijosa sought permission to transfer the debt under a new contract, the term of which was to be nine years. After several consultations the request was granted, except that the term was to

[1] *Escritura de depósito irregular*, 6 April 1839, *Archivo de Notarías*, Mexico City, vol. 720, fols. 52–4.
[2] L. Alamán and J. Guijosa to Judge, 12 March 1844, AGN, PBN, leg. 145, exp. 86.

be only five years and provided Guijosa was able to supply a guarantor of the interest. The new contract was signed on 1 April 1844.

The above negotiations were typical in most respects of the many carried out between the *Juzgado* and the prospective borrowers. Alamán was relieved of the debt by selling the property but in the majority of cases an extension was sought on the loan after the first term had expired. Although this was normally between five and nine years, the borrower was aware that when it ended an extension for a further number of years was almost certain to be granted, provided that the interest had been regularly paid. It was to the advantage of the *Juzgado* to grant extensions whenever possible for various reasons, and the terms of the contract indicate that the practice was common. In the first place, assuming the capital was still secure and the interest being paid, there was no profit to be gained by changing the investment. The rate of interest, 5 per cent, remained unchanged throughout the colonial and independence periods.

Furthermore, in spite of the contract, once money had been loaned it was difficult to retrieve. The *Juzgado* could embargo the security, and indeed all the possessions of the borrower, should the latter default in any of the clauses of the contract. However, such action involved registering a claim against the defaulter in a civil court and often engaging in a long and expensive lawsuit.[1] The *Juzgado* was naturally reluctant to take such action. For example, on 23 April 1824, Presbyter Dr D. José Vázquez obtained a loan of 22,000 pesos, using as security for this an *hacienda* which he owned in the territory of Chalco. The term of the loan was for five years and consequently on 27 August 1829 the Judge issued the customary decree as follows:

The term having expired of the contract for the investment of 22,000 pesos, which was signed and recognized on 13 April 1824, by Presbyter Dr D. José Vázquez with the special mortgage of the *hacienda* known as Our Lady of Guadalupe Tlapala in the territory of the town of

---

[1] Since 1789 most lawsuits concerning the interest or capital of *capellanías* had been heard in the civil courts, where the *Juzgado* was represented by the Legal Adviser; Judge to Minister of Justice, 16 July 1847, AGN, PBN, leg. 582, exp. 27.

Chalco, before the Public Notary D. Ignacio de la Barrera, the aforesaid Presbyter must redeem the capital within fifteen days, together
with the interest due, on the understanding that failure to do so will
result in appropriate executive action being taken.[1]

Various letters passed between Vázquez and the *Juzgado* during the
next few weeks in which the former maintained that he was not in
a position to redeem any of the debt and asked for an extension
of five years. The Judge, however, probably because the interest
had not been paid regularly, insisted that at least 4,000 pesos be
redeemed at once and if this was done an extension on the
remaining amount would be considered. This Vázquez refused to
do and the Judge ordered the matter referred to the Fiscal for his
opinion. The latter presented his report on 29 January 1830, and
he advised that the security and the guarantor of interest for the
loan were still sufficient and that Vázquez was determined to cede
the *hacienda* if he was not granted an extension on the debt. He
continued with reference to this threat that such action would
cause considerable harm to the *Juzgado*, for while the property was
in the hands of the court, which would be many years because of
the great scarcity of buyers, the interest would be paralysed for
a long period and the *hacienda* would be completely ruined, as
experience had shown constantly happened to embargoed
properties. Hence it would be most imprudent to risk this danger,
without any necessity, cause, or motive for doing so.[2] On these
grounds he recommended that the extension should be given and
the Judge gave the appropriate order on 4 February, the new
contract being signed on 12 February 1830.

In most cases the *Juzgado* would grant extensions without any
formalities or conditions. Many people inherited the debts of their
relatives and were forced to depend on the *Juzgado*'s willingness
to allow them to continue the debt. In 1839 José María Ximénes
wrote to the Judge on behalf of two clients who had inherited an
*hacienda* near Cuernavaca. Eleven years earlier the property had
been mortgaged to the extent of 14,882 pesos. The contract had
been renewed in 1833 and was now again due for renewal. The

[1] Decree of Judge, 27 August 1829, AGN, PBN, leg. 366, exp. 6.
[2] Fiscal to Judge, 29 January 1830, *ibid.*

new owners requested a further extension.[1] The Fiscal reported that the interest had been paid regularly and that there was no reason to deny the request. He added that there was no need for a new contract; all that was necessary was to endorse the old one for a further five years. The Judge issued his decree granting the extension three days later and the negotiation was therefore completed within only seven days.

In 1842 Doña Michaela Espejo wrote to the Judge to explain a similar problem. She was the tutor and guardian of her two grandsons who had inherited a house which had been mortgaged to the *Juzgado* to the extent of 12,800 pesos. She asked on their behalf for an extension of seven years on the debt.[2] The Fiscal agreed because the value of the house had increased and hence the capital remained secure.[3] The Judge issued the customary decree which was as follows:

The term of the loan is extended for five years without alteration of the previous agreement, and consequently the corresponding deed should be signed and witnessed according to the conditions normal of this *Juzgado*. It must be registered in the proper time and place, and the registrar must certify that the house has no other mortgage on it. If the latter is not the case the extension will not be considered valid.[4]

Occasionally the person owing money to the *Juzgado* was able to negotiate the terms of an extension. For example, in 1839 Miguel Osta inherited an *hacienda* in which several decades earlier the principals of various *capellanías* had been invested. No interest had been paid since 1822 and the amount owing in interest alone was 3,187 pesos. Osta offered to repay the interest debt at the rate of 400 pesos in the first month and 150 pesos every six months thereafter, and to redeem the capital owing when the estate had been settled.[5] The Fiscal refused to accept this and so Osta increased his offer to 400 in the first month and 300 half yearly. This was accepted.

---

[1] J. M. Ximénes to Judge, 24 January 1839, AGN, PBN, leg. 231, exp. 7.
[2] Doña Michaela Espejo to Judge, undated, 1842, AGN, PBN, leg. 685, exp. unmarked.
[3] Fiscal to Judge, 14 July 1842, *ibid.*
[4] Decree of Judge, 26 July 1842, *ibid.*
[5] M. Osta to Judge, undated, 1839, AGN, PBN, leg. 231, exp. 18.

Not all who borrowed money wanted to continue the debt indefinitely, for example Doña María Moreno Barrios wrote to the Judge to say that she no longer wished to continue to recognize a loan of 4,000 pesos and that she was therefore cancelling the debt by paying this amount into the *Juzgado*.[1] After confirming that the money had been received, the Judge issued the following decree:

...the Judge stated; that he determined and declared of no value the said deed as regards the capital owed. And he ordered that this should be noted in the register and the original and in the mortgage records of the territory concerned, and to this effect, an attestation of this decree should be given to the interested party.[2]

The prospective borrower knew, therefore, that once the term of the loan contract had expired he was able to redeem the debt or seek an extension on it.

As a precaution against the fact that people were sometimes unwilling to pay their debts the *Juzgado* insisted on having real estate as security for any loan. The reasons for this can be seen in the case of Diego Patrón who in 1845 sought a loan of 2,000 pesos.[3] The Fiscal presented his report on 15 May of that year and in it outlined the *Juzgado's* attitude to the security needed for a loan. Patrón had offered to guarantee the money with a personal guarantor only and had not offered any real estate as additional security. Dr Aguirre commented that on previous occasions he had expressed his opinion that pious funds should not be given out with only a guarantor as security because of the obvious risks involved and the possibility of the total loss of the capital. The *Juzgado*, he continued, was deeply convinced of the utility and positive safety which resulted from lending funds secured by a mortgage and not by personal guarantors. He illustrated his case with an example of a loan which, against his advice, had been authorized by the prelate without the additional pledge, and which had since been lost because of this. Finally he concluded that if this request was granted it would encourage all those who

[1] Doña María Barrios to Judge, undated, 1826, AGN, PBN, leg. 366, exp. 2.
[2] Decree of Judge, 9 May 1826, *ibid.*
[3] D. Patrón to Judge, 6 May 1845, AGN, PBN, leg. 284, exp. 3.

wanted to borrow money at interest from the *Juzgado* to offer only guarantors as security, and they would allege this precedent as their reason for doing so.[1]

This insistence on real estate represented a change from the terms demanded in the later colonial period, for there are many examples in the records of the *Juzgado* of loans being given without the mortgage of property. In 1771 Matías Miramontes requested and was given a loan of 100,000 pesos with only five personal guarantors.[2] It is clear that under such terms the transaction would never have been permitted in the nineteenth century. In fact, by about 1840 the *Juzgado* was in most cases relying entirely on property as the security and had ceased to demand the additional guarantors of interest.

It was also stipulated that at least two-thirds of the value of the property to be mortgaged should be free from debt, that is for a loan of 4,000 pesos the security must be worth at least 12,000 pesos.[3] In 1840 Alonso Gómez was negotiating an extension on a loan of 8,000 pesos which he had received four years earlier. The pledge he was offering was a bakery. The Fiscal commented that according to the rule constantly adhered to in the *Juzgado* the bakery should be worth at least 24,000 pesos, without including the value of equipment or stock, and that even though this two-thirds rule had been invariably followed, many pious funds were being lost.[4]

The last remark of the Fiscal is particularly significant, for in spite of the precautions being taken, considerable amounts of money were being lost. This was in part due to the difficulty in enforcing fulfilment of the terms of the contract and also because

---

[1] Fiscal to Judge, 15 May 1845, *ibid.*

[2] The documents relating to this negotiation and other similar ones are in AGN, PBN, leg. 1108, exp. 17.

[3] Alamán incorrectly states that only one-third of the value of the security needed to be free from debt: L. Alamán, *Historia de México...* (Mexico, 1849–52), vol. I, p. 68, n. 46. His mistake may have been the result of his own dealings with the *Juzgado*. In the loan which he received in 1839 he was allowed to borrow 4,000 pesos, although the house which he used as security was worth only 10,163 pesos. The Fiscal noted this fact in his report but decided to disregard the two-thirds rule, under which the security should have been valued at 12,000 pesos, because of the well-known wealth and integrity of Alamán.

[4] Fiscal to Judge, 27 November 1840, AGN, PBN, leg. 231, exp. 13.

the administrative machinery of the *Juzgado* was such that records of loan transactions were often mislaid. Furthermore, the procedure for bringing pressure to bear on those reluctant to pay was slow and largely ineffective. During the years 1825–42 the total debt in interest alone amounted to 204,563 pesos.[1] The collector pointed out regarding one debtor that he had informed the Legal Adviser on 29 September 1829. By now the same person owed interest for the past seventeen years. Nothing had been done to enforce payment during this long period and there are many other examples in which it seemed that little effort had been made to do so.

Most prospective borrowers were probably aware of this inability to enforce the contract but, nevertheless, to some the conditions imposed by the *Juzgado* were too severe. For example, if the borrower missed payment of a single instalment of interest the contract was automatically void and the creditor could proceed to take measures to embargo the security. This condition was questioned by Matías Fernández, the representative of Alonso Gómez when the latter was seeking an extension on his loan of 8,000 pesos. Fernández wrote that the condition was so severe that it could well bring ruin on anyone who accepted it completely. Although it was true that the *Juzgado*, as long as it existed in its present form, would never do anything which detracted from the benevolence for which it was so well known, nevertheless, the circumstances of the present times were so unsettled that if the ownership of the money was by some misfortune to pass into less clement hands, then the importance of the term could become grievously clear. Any temporary misfortune which afflicted the borrower could cause great harm to him and nullify the benefits which one gained by borrowing at low interest rates from the *Juzgado*. He went on to suggest that the clause be changed to the extent that the creditor could sue for the interest owing but not for the capital, until the full term of the contract had expired.[2] Needless to say, the Fiscal, in his report to the Judge, refused to

<hr/>

[1] *Lista en que se expresan los censuatorios atrazados en el pago de réditos*, 15 October 1842, AGN, PBN, leg. 685, exp. unmarked.
[2] M. Fernández to Judge, 19 September 1840, AGN, PBN, leg. 231, exp. 13.

alter a long-established clause and pointed out that a good payer need have no fear.[1] In fact, although the condition may appear to be unfair to the borrower, especially when one considers the unsettled state of the country during the first half of the nineteenth century, no case was found in the records of the *Juzgado* in which the clause was ever enforced.

In spite of, or perhaps because of, the terms described in the preceding paragraphs, the demand for loans was continuous and came from a wide variety of sources.[2] Details have already been given of Guadalupe Victoria, first president of the nation, and Lucas Alamán, a minister of influence and importance in several post independence governments, both of whom borrowed funds from the *Juzgado*. Indeed, not only a former president, but also an acting one in the person of General Barragán sought loans, the latter in 1836 being granted 4,000 pesos under the same terms as any ordinary citizen.[3] Several archbishops asked for and were given funds under the usual terms, although in 1814 Archbishop Pedro de Fonte received the sum of 20,000 pesos free of interest charges.[4] The *Juzgado* was even able to lend money to itself. The daily expenses of the employees and offices were supplied from a general fund which, particularly in the nineteenth century, was often very low. Hence in 1832 the Judge issued a decree whereby the principals of three *capellanías* amounting to 7,000 pesos were loaned to the fund.[5] Loans between individual corporations within the Church were common. The chapter in 1841 borrowed 12,000 pesos, the contract being signed and guaranteed by the Tithe Office, and the loan was redeemed twelve years later by the Tithe Accountant.[6] Most of the convents owed money to the *Juzgado* and also the hospital of San Andrés which asked for and was granted a loan of 15,000 pesos in 1817.[7]

[1] Fiscal to Judge, 27 November 1840, *ibid.*
[2] When 60,000 pesos was redeemed in the *Juzgado* in 1818, at least sixty-six people applied for loans almost immediately. These requests all survive in AGN, PBN, leg. 987, exp. 4.
[3] The documents on this negotiation are in AGN, PBN, leg. 685, exp. unmarked.
[4] Decree of Judge, 28 May 1814, AGN, PBN, leg. 800, exp. 23.
[5] Decree of Judge, 12 November 1832, AGN, PBN, leg. 27, exp. 81.
[6] The documents concerning this loan are in AGN, PBN, leg. 685, exp. unmarked.
[7] Decree of Judge, 2 October 1817, AGN, PBN, leg. 538, exp. 36.

Although still of great importance the extent of these activities was reduced in the nineteenth century because of a shortage of money. In the colonial period they had been even more widespread and influential. For example, in 1791 Viceroy Revilla Gigedo wrote to Archbishop Alonso Nuñez de Haro to request a loan from the *Juzgado* of 60,000 pesos which was to be used to buy grain to fill up the public granary. He offered as security the entire funds of the city which at that time amounted to 137,701 pesos.[1] A few years earlier, in 1783, the king had in effect assumed control of all the money in the *Juzgado* by ordering that it be deposited in the National Mint, the latter being obliged and responsible to hand over whatever amounts were required by the owners of the funds, or whenever the prelate or the Judge requested a withdrawal.[2]

The *Juzgado*, therefore, not only financed, in the words of one Minister of Justice, 'every industrious Mexican', but also kings and presidents.[3] Its activities extended throughout the archbishopric, and when one remembers that each diocese had its own *Juzgado* it is not difficult to perceive the enormous material and economic influence which was wielded by the various Judges and their advisers. However, although the institution mainly concerned with lending money on a personal basis, it was not the only one within the Church to do so. Other ecclesiastical corporations, such as the regular orders, the brotherhoods, and the colleges also invested part of their funds. Therefore, the prospective borrower was to some extent able to choose from which he wished to borrow money. The negotiation involved was similar to that of the *Juzgado* and was generally conducted with the administrator of the convent or brotherhood, who would seek permission from the *Vicario Capitular* or the prelate before granting a loan. The chief financial adviser to the diocese, known as the *Promotor Fiscal*, would also be consulted in the same way as the Fiscal in the *Juzgado*.

Two major differences are to be noted in these loan activities. In

[1] Revilla Gigedo to Archbishop, 1 June 1791, AGN, PBN, leg. 149, exp. 30.
[2] Viceroy José Gálvez to Archbishop, 20 August 1783, AGN, PBN, leg. 345, exp. 17.
[3] *Memoria del Ministro de Justicia y Negocios Eclesiástico* (1826), p. 15.

the first place the interest rate charged on personal loans was usually 6 per cent as against 5 per cent in the *Juzgado*. This and the slight divergences in the contract are probably the reasons why fewer people sought loans from this source. Secondly, voluntarily or otherwise, the convents and monasteries were often involved in loans to public corporations, and, as already indicated, after independence they furnished large amounts to several civil governments. The reason for this lies in the nature of the finances of the respective corporations. With the exception of its general fund the *Juzgado* administered but did not own any of the capital it loaned. On the other hand, most of the wealth of the regular orders came from legacies, alms, and rents of properties, and subject to the approval of the prelate, each convent could dispose of it as it wished. Therefore, the burden of government loans fell on the convents who were more easily able to raise the required amounts by the sale of property and the use of uncommitted funds.

The same reasons enabled the regular orders to amass large amounts of capital and they were consequently concerned more than the *Juzgado* with loans to corporations, for example, the Royal Tribunal of Mining. In 1800 the latter sought a loan of 80,000 pesos at $4\frac{1}{2}$ per cent interest from the convent of La Concepción. The request was referred to the prelate who in turn sent it to his adviser. The latter's report indicates why this type of loan was preferred:

The investment is useful and secure, for although private citizens might be able to pay 5 per cent interest they could not offer the security which the Tribunal and its rents provide. Also it would be difficult to find individuals with sufficient wealth to need and be able to guarantee a loan of 80,000 pesos, and a tardy investment would mean that the capital would be without yield for some time.[1]

The Archbishop accepted the report and decreed that the money should be loaned to the Tribunal at $4\frac{1}{2}$ per cent.

Another interesting loan was made by the convent of San Bernardo in 1817. The Jesuit Order had been allowed to return to the country but had not been given back the properties and funds

---

[1] *Promotor Fiscal* to Archbishop, undated, 1800, AGN, PBN, leg. 1786, exp. 1.

which had been confiscated in 1767, with the exception of the *hacienda* of San José Acolman. Pedro Cantón, head of the province at this time, wrote to the prelate explaining how he lacked sufficient finance to re-establish the Order and asked permission to borrow 8,000 pesos at 5 per cent from the convent of San Bernardo, using as security the one *hacienda* which the Jesuits now possessed.[1] The request was granted and a loan given for a term of five years.

Personal loans were given on terms similar to those of the *Juzgado* and to the same kind of person. In 1850 José María González de la Vega wrote to the *Vicario Capitular* on behalf of José Joaquín de Herrera, President of the Republic, to ask for a loan of 3,000 pesos from the funds of the *Colegio de Tepotzotlan*, which he knew were to be invested.[2] The financial adviser to whom the request was referred found everything in order and recommended acceptance of the proposed loan. The *Vicario Capitular* consequently ordered that the money be given and the contract was signed on 15 May 1850.

Loans were also given to citizens less eminent than the president. In 1859 two ladies, Doña Carmen and Doña Tirsa Piña, received 2,000 pesos from *La Concepción* which they needed to cover a similar amount owing to the convent of *Antigua Enseñanza*.[3] As in the colonial period, requests were often received from the parents of novices who were unable to afford the dowry of 4,000 pesos which had to be paid when the final vows were taken. The problem of finding the amount was frequently solved by theoretically borrowing the 4,000 pesos from the convent and using it to pay the dowry.[4] In fact, no money changed hands but the parents recognized the debt. Loans were likewise given to finance small business ventures or to improve property. In 1845 Tomás López Pimentel, a senator in the General Congress,

[1] P. Cantón to Archbishop, undated, 1817, AGN, PBN, leg. 82, exp. 70.
[2] J. M. González de la Vega to *Vicario Capitular*, undated, 1850, AGN, PBN, leg. 121, exp. unmarked.
[3] The documents concerning this loan are in AGN, PBN, leg. 1786, exp. 1.
[4] For example, see *Expediente promovido por D. José Guerrero sobre que se reconozcan sobre su casa los 4000 pesos de la dote de su hija Sor. Rafaela, novicia del convento de la Concepción*, AGN, PBN, leg. 145, exp. unmarked.

borrowed 2,000 pesos from the convents of *La Nueva* and *La Antigua Enseñanza* in order to develop his business interests.[1]

Procedure similar to that of the *Juzgado* was followed with reference to extensions and redemptions of loans. An unusual case arose in 1828 when José María Fagoaga wrote to the administrator of the convent of *San Jerónimo* admitting that he owed them several sums of money. He asked that a house should be accepted in part payment of these debts. The administrator, Manuel Pajalaguna, reported the proposals to the *Vicario de Religiosas*, but then sent a second confidential letter in which he began by saying that he had not previously disclosed certain facts because considerable inconvenience would be caused if they were publicly known, and particularly if Fagoaga learned of them.[2] He had discovered that the contract signed by Fagoaga had only two guarantors and no real estate as security. Also the convent's copies of the contract had been lost, with the result that if the borrower's goods were embargoed and a meeting of creditors arranged, the claims of the convent would be worthless. He therefore urged that the house offered by Fagoaga be accepted immediately before the latter discovered the reality of his position. The *Vicario de Religiosas* ordered acceptance of the property and that the contract should be drawn up immediately.

It is clear, therefore, that the investment and loan activities of the Church were extensive. The *Juzgado*, and to a lesser extent the regular orders, acted as lending banks from which any property-owning person could borrow money at a reasonable rate of interest. There were no other similar credit institutions which could offer an almost continuous supply of finance to the aspiring businessmen and merchants in the country. Some of such borrowers, who were almost entirely dependent on the Church for financial assistance, are mentioned in the following passage:

An owner of a mine which looks promising, who is sinking the first shaft, or constructing a tunnel, or a drain, or some other unproductive work, when his money runs out, if he has a few friends who are willing to serve as guarantors or a property he can mortgage, he can borrow the capital he needs from pious funds...

[1] The documents concerning this are in AGN, PBN, leg. 1150, exp. 47.
[2] M. Pajalaguna to *Vicario de Religiosas*, 24 January 1828, AGN, PBN, leg. 145, exp. 82.

The businessman who is beginning his career with only limited capital, can increase it with funds from pious works; the man who, because of some misfortune, could not sell all his goods and whose creditors are demanding settlement and threatening attachment which could finish his business interests and reduce his credit worthiness and reputation, he can avoid these problems by using a loan from pious funds...

Similar benefits from pious funds are enjoyed by builders, artisans, and other merchants; everyone in fact who, because of misfortune and accidents, has found himself in financial difficulty.[1]

The general significance and importance of the capital invested by the Church is lucidly illustrated in the writings of Bishop Abad y Queipo, who in 1805 protested so strongly against the implementation of the laws of consolidation. He maintained that the withdrawal of clerical capital from the country would have ruinous effects on the economy, for in his estimation clerical funds represented two-thirds of the productive capital then in circulation. The numerical calculations of the bishop were probably incorrect but complaints in the country as a whole were often made that the Church exercised a virtual monopoly of credit. The Church did not deny this fact. It was the only institution with sufficient funds to act as a lending bank and therefore it did so. To suggestions that these banking activities should be put in the hands of the State or private individuals, the Church had a very reasonable answer, put explicitly by the bishop of Puebla in 1829:

This is precisely what the Church does and without expensive costs: its coffers and treasuries are banks which are better placed and organized than anything that could be proposed: they are sources of common prosperity, where the businessman and the farmer find the needed funds to help them out of their difficulties, and give them the opportunity to make some gain. Why remove so experienced a resource of agriculture and commerce? Why substitute it by another, of which the inconveniences are evident and the results at least entirely doubtful?[2]

---

[1] *Exposición del cabildo de México al Exmo. Vicepresidente D. Anastasio Bustamante...*, February 1830; publ. in *Colección eclesiástica mexicana* (Mexico, 1834), vol. IV, pp. 64–5.

[2] *Exposición del cabildo de Puebla...sobre el decreto de Zacatecas relativo al establecimiento de un banco con los caudales piadosos*, 17 March 1830; publ. in *Colección eclesiástica mexicana*, vol. IV, p. 79.

## Personal Loans from the 'Juzgado'

An impartial examination of the documentary evidence must lead one to the conclusion that the activities of the Church in the sphere of personal loans provided an essential service and that the monopoly of credit exercised by the clergy was not abused in any way. The *Juzgado* charged only 5 per cent simple interest and did not take advantage of any temporary financial embarrassment which the borrower may have experienced. Most of the writers who have criticized the loan activities of the Church have ignored the fact that the *Juzgado* was a purely administrative organization whose function and responsibility were to safeguard the funds entrusted to it by individual citizens. The duty of the Judge and his officials was to implement the instructions given to them by the founders of benefices and pious works, and the investment policy practised by the Church was considered the best means of fulfilling its obligations.

# CHAPTER 4

# THE EFFECTS OF
# CLERICAL INVESTMENT

The amounts invested by the ecclesiastical corporations are difficult to ascertain. The examples of loans given in the preceding chapters are only a few of the many thousands contained in the Church records which clearly reveal that the total capital invested by way of personal loans amounted to several millions of pesos. Numerous calculations have been made of the total wealth of the Church in Mexico but most of these estimates are unreliable because of bias, and none seems to have been based on primary sources. Cuevas has indicated the inaccuracies of those most frequently quoted.[1] For example, with regard to Alamán, who stated that the Church owned at least half the real estate in the country, Cuevas points out that according to Alamán's own statistics, the total capital value of real estate was in the region of 4,000 million pesos and that no one had dared to say that the clergy owned 2,000 million pesos worth of land. Such an estimate was clearly incorrect. Again the estimates made by the liberal Mora come under Cuevas's scrutiny. He rightly notes several basic errors, for example Mora calculated the tithe revenue on the basis of the 1829 returns and ignored the fact that since the 1833 law, the yield had greatly decreased. He also ignores the fact that more than half the tithe product was paid to the civil authorities. Mora's estimate of the total productive capital of the Church amounted to 149,131,460 pesos, but in arriving at this he in effect misused his figures. For example, he capitalized the tithe revenue on the basis that this equalled a 5 per cent yield, and hence included as a productive

[1] M. Cuevas, *Historia de la Iglesia en México*, 5th ed. (Mexico, 1947), vol. v, chapter I, book III. Attempts were made to compile accurate accounts by several ministers, but all were unsuccessful; for example, in 1828 the Minister of Justice tried to ascertain the value of the *capellanías* in each diocese. The table which was begun but never completed is in AGN, *Justicia Eclesiástica*, vol. 23, fol. 85. This shows the number and value of *capellanías* in the sees of Puebla, Guadalajara, Valladolid, Monterey, Oaxaca and Yucatan. The space left for the archbishopric is blank.

capital the sum of 46,823,040 pesos. The tithe revenue cannot be considered a capital asset for the Church, for it only received the product and had no proprietary claims on the capital. Similarly, to capitalize revenue from alms, as Mora does, is a purely theoretical exercise and in reality impossible. Cuevas details other inaccuracies in Mora's calculations and those of other writers. His main general complaint is that countless authors have produced a great variety of estimates with apparently no evidence on which to base them. They are pure guesses. Unfortunately, Cuevas, ignoring the available documentary records of tithe income, rents, and *capellanías*, proceeded to make his own guess based on a few printed contemporary accounts, which suited the low estimate he wished to make. Fortunately, some accurate idea of the amounts involved within the archdiocese does emerge from several documents found among the records of the *Juzgado* and the convents.

One is an account which lists in alphabetical order the names of borrowers, the amounts loaned to each one, and the dates on which the contracts were signed.[1] The document itself is undated but many of the loans noted were given after 1800, the last one indicated being 1821. According to this account the total amount of the *Juzgado*'s investments was approximately 4,244,000 pesos. This figure can be supported by reference to other accounts. Between the beginning of 1817 and October 1819 the *Juzgado* paid out the sum of 322,915 pesos in interest on benefices.[2] From this figure must be deducted the sum of 8,658 which was embezzled and fraudulently given out by an employee, which leaves a total of 314,257. On average this equals a monthly sum of 14,965 and an annual total of 179,580. This latter figure represents 5 per cent of the capital value of the foundations, which means that the principal value amounted to 3,591,600 pesos, that is 652,400 pesos less than the amount taken from the list of borrowers. The difference in the two figures may be explained as follows: benefices to the value of over 300,000 pesos on the list are noted as being established

---

[1] To be found in AGN, PBN, leg. 27, exp. 78.
[2] From a document dealing with the fraudulent theft of money by one of the *Juzgado*'s employees, AGN, PBN, leg. 991, exp. 17.

after 1819, and therefore no interest could have been paid on these. Secondly, vacant *capellanías* probably account for the remaining difference of 350,000.[1] The interest on vacant benefices would not of course be paid out. Hence it can be assumed that the current active capital invested by the *Juzgado* at the beginning of the independence period was a little over four million pesos.

The amounts invested by the other ecclesiastical corporations are also difficult to estimate with any accuracy. No general accounts seem to have survived among documentary sources, and the only ones available are those sent to the Minister of Justice and occasionally published by him in his annual report.[2] These, however, only concern the regular orders and not the many colleges, brotherhoods, and charitable institutions supported by the Church. For example, in a table drawn up by the Minister in 1843, the convents within the archiepiscopal jurisdiction are shown to have investments to the value of 1,665,925 pesos active capital, which returned an annual interest of 82,466 pesos. In addition, more than one million pesos is noted as passive capital returning no interest.[3] These tables were formed by the Minister from data sent to him by convents and can be presumed to show minimum amounts, for no convent, particularly in the nineteenth century, would have overstated its own wealth.

The figures given above serve to show that the investment activity of the Church was extensive. Every kind of real estate was mortgaged. One list of properties which owed money to the *Juzgado* included in addition to private dwellings the following commercial enterprises: a tannery, a tavern, a butcher's shop, a bakery, and a factory making rum.[4] Many of the mortgage debts dated from the eighteenth century and the money had been

---

[1] In 1805 the capital value of vacant *capellanías* was 556,960 pesos; this figure is from a list in AGN, PBN, leg. 958, exp. 32.

[2] For example, see *Memoria del Ministro de Justicia y Negocios Eclesiásticos* (1828), estado no. 14.

[3] *Estado general y circunstanciado de los conventos de religiosas existentes en la república mexicana*, 31 December 1843, AGN, *Justicia Eclesiástica*, vol. 144, fol. 375. Passive capital consisted mainly of the funds confiscated under the laws of consolidation, and of loans which had been given to institutions, for example the *Consulados* and the *Tribunal de la Minería*, which had subsequently been abolished.

[4] Account headed *Casas* in AGN, PBN, leg. 27, exp. 78.

allowed to remain invested even though several changes of ownership must have occurred. Rural property was in a similar situation. The account shown overleaf and sent to the prelate by the priest in the parish of Tulancingo shows the extent of the debts owed to the Church within a single parish.

Other accounts reveal the same situation, for example one entitled *Haciendas* and another *Ranchos* list rural properties which owed money to the *Juzgado*. Again much of the capital had remained invested for several generations.[1] Property was so extensively affected by this investment because, as indicated in the previous chapter, the personal loans given by the *Juzgado* and the convents were almost invariably guaranteed by real estate, with the result that the Church exercised a dominant and almost complete control of the land within the archbishopric, and indeed, the country. The allegedly detrimental effects of this clerical investment provided one of the main issues in Mexican political and economic thought in the nineteenth century and were an essential factor determining liberal hostility towards Church wealth as a whole.

Among the harmful effects was that affirmed by Miguel Lerdo de Tejada in 1856 in a circular in which he sought to justify his law disamortizing clerical property.[2] He wrote that the decree was going to end one of the economic deficiencies which had most contributed to preventing the circulation of property, that is the possession of so much theoretically inalienable real estate in the hands of the Church. Although he was referring specifically to houses and farms owned directly by the ecclesiastical corporations, as opposed to those controlled by mortgages, it was generally believed that this, together with clerical investment, had caused the movement of property to stop. This view was reasonable but in many respects incorrect. It was based first on the ecclesiastical laws of mortmain, and secondly on the fact that the personal loans given by the Church were guaranteed by property.

[1] These accounts are in AGN, PBN, leg. 27, exp. 78.

[2] *Circular con que D. Miguel Lerdo de Tejada, Ministro de Hacienda y Crédito Público acompañó la ley sobre desamortización de fincas rústicas y urbanas, propiedad de corporaciones civiles y religiosas,* 28 June 1856; publ. in M. L. Guzmán (ed.), *Leyes de reforma,* 2nd ed. (Mexico, 1955), pp. 37–42.

| Principal | Interest | Borrowers | Mortgages | Object |
|---|---|---|---|---|
| 3,000 | 150 | B. D. Manuel Cabofranco | Hacienda de Exguitlan | Parish school |
| 3,750 | 187.4 | Idem | Idem | Masses |
| 300 | 15 | D. Juan Oropeza | His house | Burial fees |
| 1,020 | 51 | Da. Ma. Nieves Muruniondo | Her house | Masses |
| 1,040 | 52 | D. José Zeron | Land | Masses |
| 200 | 10 | D. José Elizalde | Hacienda de Hueypan | Idem |
| 60 | 3 | D. Antonio Montero | His house | Idem |
| 300 | 15 | Lic. D. José Soto | Idem | Idem |
| 180 | 9 | Idem | Idem | Idem |
| 800 | 40 | B. D. Rafael Fernández | Rancho de Huatenco | Idem |
| 180 | 9 | Da. Rita Manilla | Her hacienda | Idem |
| 120 | 6 | D. José M. Ferreros | His house | Idem |
| 600 | 30 | Da. María Ferreros | Idem | Novena |
| 300 | 15 | Da. Francisca Alfaro | Her house | |
| 300 | 15 | Las Llados | Their house | Masses |
| 360 | 18 | D. José Ochoa | His house | Idem |
| 1,000 | 50 | Idem | Idem | Idem |
| 200 | 10 | Idem | Idem | Idem |
| 400 | 20 | Idem | Idem | Idem |
| 100 | 5 | Idem | Idem | Idem |
| 500 | 25 | Idem | Idem | Idem |
| 340 | 17 | Idem | Idem | Idem |
| 120 | 6 | Idem | Idem | Idem |
| 240 | 12 | D. Mariano Sánchez | His house | Idem |
| 1,000 | 50 | D. Mariano Ocariz | Hacienda de Huapalcalco | Idem |
| 130 | 4 | Da. Guadalupe Brito | Her house | Idem |
| 1,200 | 60 | D. Ignacio Soto | His house | Idem |
| 80 | 4 | Da. Mariana Ayluardo | Idem | Idem |
| 180 | 9 | Idem | Idem | Idem |
| 3,000 | 150 | Consolidation | 000 | Capellanía[1] with 12 masses |

[1] *Estado que manifiesta los caudales de obras pías que se reconocen a favor de la parroquia de Tulancingo, con expresión de los censuatorios, hipotecas, y objeto de sus réditos...*, 1817, AGN, PBN, leg. 82, exp. 73.

It was often assumed that, according to the laws of mortmain, once the Church had acquired possession of a property the latter under no circumstances could be alienated or disposed of. The vast number of houses owned by the Church were therefore considered to be withdrawn from circulation. In 1834 the provincial of Carmen wrote a long article to dispel this erroneous view.[1] The ecclesiastical corporations, according to the provincial, were perfectly entitled to sell their goods, and by so doing contravened no civil or canon law. Even the sale of holy ornaments was permitted provided that the institution involved could prove either a definite advantage in the sale, or an absolute need for it. The person to decide whether the latter requirements were met was the prelate, or in the case of a vacant see, the governing chapter. The provincial wrote this article precisely because the Church was selling its property and was being attacked for doing so.

Contrary to the view that clerical property was immobile, there is no doubt that the Church did sell many of its houses after independence. As will be shown in detail later, the clergy came to the conclusion, after the attempted liberal reform of 1833, that the investment of capital provided better security than the possession of easily confiscated real estate, and that in accordance with this new policy the regular orders and the *Juzgado* began to sell their properties. Also in later years the constant demands of the government for loans led to the need to raise large amounts of capital, and many corporations were only able to do so by the sale of their goods. The greatest indication that clerical property was circulating lies in the fact that successive governments found it necessary to issue decrees and circulars ordering the sales to stop or at least be controlled. Such measures as these were decreed on 20 November 1833, 24 January, 9 July 1834, 4 August 1838, 27 June 1842, and 3 February 1843. Usually they ordered that permission for the sale of any clerical property had to be obtained from the civil authority, but this restriction was ineffective, for virtually every request to sell a house seems to have been granted.

---

[1] *Exposición que el Provincial del Carmen hizo al Supremo Gobierno sobre las ventas de fincas que celebraron algunos conventos de su orden* (Mexico, 1834).

The fact that there are many hundreds, and perhaps thousands, of such requests among the records of the Ministry of Justice again contradicts the allegation that Church ownership of real estate restricted or prevented the circulation of property.[1] Indeed, it is possible that the purpose of the above-mentioned laws was to ensure that the Church retained its houses. The first of the decrees was imposed in 1833, according to the preamble, because ecclesiastical property and funds were being squandered and wasted.[2] It seems likely that the motive was more subtle. The governments must have realized that if the Church was allowed to divest itself of its real estate holdings in favour of invested capital, then loans to the State could no longer be mortgaged to Church property. As long as the ecclesiastical corporations were in possession of real estate, the civil authorities could persuade financiers to lend funds to the government by guaranteeing repayment with clerical property. Almost all Church–State loans after independence were negotiated on this basis. The government would issue bills which were bought by financial speculators. Repayment of the bills at a later date was made by the Church, which guaranteed redemption by mortgaging its goods. It seems clear that no person would buy government bills if they were secured by only the invested capital of the Church, for experience had shown that it was very difficult to retrieve invested funds which were in the hands of the general public.

Hence clerical ownership of real estate did not prevent the circulation of property. However, the Church was in a position to do so, mainly because of the investment policy practised by the *Juzgado* and the regular orders. The *Juzgado* loan contract contained a clause referring to the real estate security of which the following is an example:

...the six houses, together with everything in and belonging to them, with no exception, must not be sold, ceded, given, pledged, nor in any other way disposed of until the said capital has been redeemed and the interests paid.[3]

[1] For example, see AGN, *Justicia Eclesiástica*, vols. 126, 149, 165.
[2] Dublán y Lozano, II, 635.
[3] *Escritura de reconocimiento*, 14 April 1822, AGN, PBN, leg. 230, exp. 66.

The contracts signed by those who borrowed from the regular orders contained a similar condition, for example:

...the said house constitutes the mortgage, together with everything which in fact and in law corresponds to it, and it must not be sold, pledged, nor in any other way disposed of, so long as this credit subsists.[1]

Almost every personal loan given by the Church in the nineteenth century was under conditions similar to the above. Hence the owner of a house or farm, by assuming a mortgage on his property, handed over complete control of it to the ecclesiastical creditor who was empowered to restrict and prevent any change in tenure. If the Church had insisted on the strict observance of the terms of the contract, then property could have been completely immobilized. It did not do so and there is ample documentary evidence to prove that mortgaged property circulated relatively freely.

For example, two courses of action were open to the owner of a mortgaged house if he wished to sell the property. In the first instance he could redeem the loan, in which case he was free to negotiate a selling price with any prospective purchaser. Alternatively, he could agree with the buyer that the latter should continue to recognize the debt and to pay the interest on it, in which case the selling price would be reduced by a sum equivalent to the amount to be recognized by the new owner. The latter course was mostly adopted. In 1846 Licenciado D. Diego de la Peña, representing Fernández Barrera, wrote to the Judge to apply for permission to sell a house belonging to his client. The property had been mortgaged to the *Juzgado* to the amount of 9,275 pesos but the prospective buyer had agreed that the debt should be transferred to him.[2] The Judge referred the matter to the Fiscal who found everything in order and recommended that the sale be allowed, provided the buyer signed a new loan contract. A similar case occurred in 1830 when Manuel López Ocampo wrote to the Judge to ask permission to buy a house and to continue to recognize the capital fund of a *capellanía* which had been invested

[1] *Escritura de reconocimiento*, 14 June 1856, AGN, PBN, leg. 125, exp. 5.
[2] Diego de la Peña to Judge, undated, 1846, AGN, PBN, leg. 582, exp. 20.

in it.[1] The Fiscal again advised acceptance of the proposal and noted that the money had remained invested in the same property since 1797.

Occasionally the buyer stipulated that the property should be free from debt, in which case the seller was sometimes able to transfer the mortgage to another house. Agustín Carpena had used four houses which he owned as security for a loan of 2,000 pesos, and now wished to sell one of them. In order to free it from debt in accordance with the demands of the purchaser, he asked that the mortgage should be reduced to the three remaining houses.[2] In his report on the proposal the Fiscal considered that the loan would still be secure under the reduced guarantee and that therefore the request should be allowed.

The same procedure was involved in the sale of mortgaged rural property. In 1839 José Medina asked permission to sell an *hacienda* on which he owed 4850 pesos and for the new owner to assume the debt. The request was granted and the sale completed.[3] A person would even buy a farm on the assumption that he would be allowed to keep the mortgage. In 1800 Rafael Rivera informed the Judge that he had purchased the *hacienda* of San Miguel from Joaquín de Aldana for a price of 35,045 pesos, of which he had paid 20,000 in cash. Of the remaining 15,045 pesos, Aldana owed to the *Juzgado* all but 2,812 pesos, and Rivera requested that responsibility for the whole amount be transferred to himself. Again the request was allowed.[4]

From the above examples and many others examined among ecclesiastical records, it is clear that clerical investment did not prevent the movement of property, because the *Juzgado* and the regular orders rarely used the power given to them by the terms of the contract. If they had done so the result would have been as Dr Mora alleged in his several works concerning the influence of Church wealth on the economic development of the country. He

---

[1] M. López Ocampo to Judge, undated, 1830, AGN, PBN, leg. 967, exp. 10.

[2] A. Carpena to Judge, undated, 1847, AGN, PBN, leg. 582, exp. 32.

[3] The documents concerning this negotiation are in AGN, PBN, leg. 231, exp. 10. An unusual feature of this case was that Medina was granted a personal interview with the Fiscal before the latter presented his report to the Judge.

[4] For this negotiation, see AGN, PBN, leg. 175, exp. 2.

maintained, and innumerable subsequent authors have followed his opinions, that the investment activities of the clergy had brought real estate and agriculture to a state of bankruptcy.[1] The war of independence had a disastrous effect on rural property. Crops were ruined, implements broken, and agricultural production decreased. With the Church owning a large part of the capital in circulation and having some claim on most farms, one would at first think that the war would have been ruinous to the clergy. Certainly little interest can have been paid by many farmers on the capital borrowed from the Church, and the value of land dropped as a result of the long war, but, in the opinion of Mora, this was to the advantage of the ecclesiastical creditor. He argued that owners who before the independence war had maintained their properties with a mortgage superior, equal, or just less than the value of the house, found that after the war had ended they were still faced with the same mortgage, even though their property was only worth half its former value, or even less. The result was that they were unable to pay the interest on the mortgage and their houses were almost all embargoed.[2]

Certainly the war did cause much hardship and many people found themselves in financial difficulties. For example, Felipe Martínez owed 1,000 pesos to a priest and in 1813 he wrote that he had been trying to sell his carriage in order to raise some money to pay off the debt. He pointed out, however, that because of the circumstances of the day, and the common misfortune which affected everybody, he had been unable to find anyone who could even make an offer.[3]

According to Mora, the Church disregarded the inevitable poverty resulting from the long war and claimed all unpaid interest, maintaining that the debts owing in 1810 were still owing in 1821 and after. Furthermore, the new occupants of the properties which were embargoed assumed the capital debt which they had no hope of paying. Successive owners were ruined by the

[1] J. M. L. Mora, 'Agricultura nacional: estado de bancarrota a que se halla reducida', *Boletín de Agricultura* (Mexico, 1846), pp. 109–14. This article was based on an earlier essay included in Mora's work *México y sus revoluciones*, first published in Paris, 1836.
[2] *Ibid.* p. 110.
[3] F. Martínez to R. P. F. Luis Carrasco, 13 December 1813, AGN, PBN, leg. 92, exp. 39.

debt, which many made worse by adding the unpaid interest to the capital debt thus raising the amount of interest to be paid even higher. The inevitable result was that most owners sooner or later were driven to bankruptcy in their efforts to repay the clergy.

To Mora this situation was clearly unjust and uneconomic. He pointed out that although the ownership of a farm might be in the name of an individual, the real owner was in fact almost always the Church, because in a large number of properties all the capital value belonged to the Church, and in almost all others the ecclesiastical corporations owned the greater part. This gave the clergy a notable advantage, for they were not exposed to the risks and losses which were so common and probable in times of political disturbances. Such losses always fell on the titular owner of the property and usually resulted in his ruin.[1]

These criticisms by Dr Mora cannot be wholly justified in view of the evidence revealed by a study of the available documentation. It has already been indicated that the *Juzgado*, which was the main investor, insisted at least in the nineteenth century that two-thirds of the value of the house or farm to be mortgaged must be free from debt, that is, for a loan of 4,000 pesos the property must be worth 12,000 pesos. Mora's argument was that real estate values had so decreased that a farm, mortgaged to the sum of 4,000 pesos and formerly worth 12,000 pesos, was after 1821 valued at less than 4,000 pesos and thus completely controlled by the ecclesiastical creditor. In some cases this must indeed have happened, but only in relation to those properties which were already mortgaged before or during the war of independence. In many instances farms may have been made entirely unproductive by the effects of the war, but this situation cannot have been as widespread or general as alleged by Mora, for otherwise agricultural production would have come to a virtual halt. The tithe yields within the archbishopric, which to some extent provide a guide to the amount of agricultural produce, certainly reveal a decline after 1821 but this is only gradual and not immediately severe. There seems no evidence to justify Mora's estimate of the decline in

[1] Mora, *Boletín de Agricultura*, p. 113.

property values. Furthermore, Mora pays no attention to the fact that many thousands of loans were given after 1821 and these were almost invariably guaranteed by a house or farm, two-thirds of the value of which was free from debt. Hence, in thousands of properties the ecclesiastical creditor in fact owned only one-third of the capital value. Another factor ignored by Mora was the change in real estate values. Prices may have dropped during the war, and perhaps for some time afterwards, but by 1839 prices in some cases were rising. The Fiscal in a report on a proposed loan recommended that the house offered as security was sufficient, particularly because the value of urban property was rising daily.

Mora, who was the chief liberal spokesman on these matters, was incorrect in other of his allegations. He wrote that the capitalists did not buy properties. Those people that did so, because of the mortgage debt, had to pay a price much higher than the true value and were therefore liable for high interest payments. They were unable to meet the interest because they could not acquire the necessary capital to carry out improvements and increase production, because the capitalists preferred to use their funds in other ways, for example, in loans to the State. Even in those cases where the new owners acquired their properties by simply assuming the mortgage and paying no cash, they were prevented from investing any money they had in improvements because the term of the mortgage was always very short and never exceeded six years. The creditor could demand the redemption of the capital owed before any advantage or profit could be realized from the improvements. Redemption would not yet be possible, and therefore the property would be embargoed and money invested in new equipment and machinery would be lost.[1]

These points can all easily be disproved. It has been clearly shown in the preceding chapter that the *Juzgado* and the regular orders were willing to, and in practice did, grant extensions on their loans, many of which were for initial terms of up to nine years. Therefore, a person was able to carry out improvements, not under the threat of having to repay a loan within a few years, but in the almost certain knowledge that he would be allowed to

---

[1] *Ibid.* p. 111.

retain the capital which he had borrowed. Indeed, contrary to preventing improvements, it was to the creditor's advantage that they should be carried out, for the property would then increase in value and the investment would be more secure. Any property to be used as security had to have at least two-thirds of its value free from debt before any loan could be authorized. This condition encouraged prospective borrowers to improve their properties. For example, in 1845 Nicolás Domínguez wrote to the Judge to explain that he wished to buy a house and to assume the mortgage already on it of 3,000 pesos. The property was now valued at only 5,000 pesos, and therefore, to conform with the two-thirds rule, he offered to carry out repairs and generally raise the value to 9,000 pesos.[1] The Fiscal recommended acceptance of the proposal provided Domínguez guaranteed to finish the work within one year. He agreed and having completed the stipulated improvements within the year was allowed to assume the debt.

In 1845 Manuel Piña y Cuevas bought the *hacienda* San José el Grande and in the purchase price had assumed a mortgage debt of 80,854 pesos. In November he wrote to the Judge to ask for a further loan of 3,000 pesos to finance the building of an irrigation plant which would increase the productivity of the property and add to the improvements which he had already carried out.[2] The Fiscal advised that the loan should be given but only on condition that the plant should be built within a given time. The work was completed quickly and the loan was granted.

As has been stated, it was in the interests of the Church that those who borrowed clerical funds should put them to productive use and so enable themselves to pay the agreed interest. It was definitely not clerical policy to appropriate properties for debt. Nothing was to be gained by the creditor in changing the investment so long as it remained secure and the interest was paid. This attitude was well illustrated in the case of Juan de Dios Pradel whose wife inherited the *hacienda* La Borja and several surrounding properties. The estates were in bad repair and owed a considerable amount of money. Pradel asked the Judge for an extension on these

[1] N. Domínguez to Judge, 10 March 1845, AGN, PBN, leg. 284, exp. 10.
[2] M. Piña y Cuevas to Judge, 20 November 1845, AGN, PBN, leg. 284, exp. 13.

debts because he maintained that since he had assumed the management and administration of the properties the land and produce had greatly increased in value. He remitted an account showing the financial situation; the estates as a whole had been recently valued at 300,625 pesos and the total debt on them was 107,240 pesos, of which 40,700 was owed to the *Juzgado* and the remainder to various convents. The interest on the total debt was now being paid with the income received from renting several small farms on the estate.[1] He was clearly unable to redeem the debt. The Fiscal reported that the only solution seemed to be to grant an extension of nine years and thus avoid the necessity of having to embargo the properties in order to recover the capital owed. He pointed out that an embargo would cause considerable harm, for insolvency proceedings lasted for many years, and often ended in the loss of both capital and interest.[2] On the basis of this report the request for an extension was granted. Some five years later, however, the estate was appropriated and although the documentation on the matter does not reveal the cause of this action it is evident from the words of the Fiscal that the *Juzgado*, which was the largest single creditor, was not eager for such a course to be adopted.

There were occasions on which the *Juzgado* or the convents decided that the only way to safeguard the clerical funds was to embargo the property and in effect sue the owner for debt. No exceptions were apparently made in such cases, for properties belonging to Ignacio de la Campa y Coz, an employee of the *Juzgado* in 1813, were adjudicated by a civil court to the institution in payment of pious funds and interest that had been borrowed.[3] There are similar examples among the records of the *Juzgado* and they must have been more frequent in earlier periods, for in the eighteenth century the Property Administrator was known as 'Receiver of embargoed properties' (*Depositario de fincas embargadas*). In the accounts of this latter employee for the year 1791, however, only fourteen properties were being managed by him

[1] Juan de Dios Pradel to Judge, 1 July 1845, AGN, PBN, leg. 284, exp. 6.
[2] Fiscal to Judge, 18 July 1845, *ibid.*
[3] *Hacedurá Pública* to Judge, 7 September 1820, AGN, PBN, leg. 85, exp. 61.

and the number never increased in the nineteenth century beyond fifty.[1] The Legal Adviser employed to attend to embargoes was increasingly occupied during the nineteenth century, but his accounts show that the *Juzgado* was not involved in a great number of these disputes. The convents also sued people for debt but again there seems to be no evidence to substantiate the charges made by Mora that the courts were continuously filled with cases in which the Church was appropriating property for debt.[2]

Mora also condemns the division of the land. Part of the value of owning a large estate in the sixteenth century depended upon the number of Indians who were attached to it, and with the scarcity of population at that time the property had to be widespread in order to encompass sufficient Indians within its territory. The value of the *hacienda* was now in its produce, because with the rise in population and consumption the demand for agricultural products greatly increased. But with the *hacienda* being so extensive, a large part of it was often uncultivated and unproductive. This Mora blames on the investment activities of the Church, for he maintains that, when the value of the land increased, many of the owners would have been willing to sell parts of their estates which were not productive. They were unable to do this because the land was mortgaged for loans already contracted with the Church, which was unwilling to see the guarantee divided, with the subsequent complications regarding the capital already lent on the land. The landowner, as long as he was in possession of his vast property, knew that he could easily obtain further loans from the clergy. Finally Mora claimed that in many cases, if the estates were divided and split up into smaller units, they would be able to bear the mortgage debt, which as a single unit they were unable to do.[3]

Although there is no documentary evidence to prove or disprove the latter allegations, it does seem probable that the ecclesiastical corporations which invested money in property would not be eager to allow the security to be divided. Neverthe-

---

[1] These accounts are in AGN, PBN, leg. 910, exp. 8.
[2] Mora, *Boletín de Agricultura*, pp. 111–12.
[3] Mora, *Boletín de Agricultura*, p. 112.

less, the hypothesis stated by Mora that the landowner might have been willing to sell the unproductive parts of his estates seems unlikely, for the amount of money loaned on the land depended on its value, which in turn depended on its produce. It was in the interest of the landowner to make the unproductive land productive and thereby increase the value of his properties, which would enable him to borrow even greater amounts.

It is interesting to note the attitude of the Cathedral chapter of the diocese of Puebla:

> The ecclesiastical chapter still recognizes as an unquestionable principle of rural economy, that the accumulation of many and large properties in the possession of a single owner is an insuperable obstacle to the progress of agriculture.[1]

In spite of this statement it is perhaps significant that a large part of the property confiscated from the Jesuits in 1767 was purchased by only one person, the Count of Regla. On 26 May 1783 he brought 'haciendas, houses, and mines' for the sum of 767,571 pesos. Most of this purchase price was borrowed from the ecclesiastical corporations.[2]

No definitive conclusion can be reached concerning the effects of clerical investment on the division of the land, but there is little doubt that it was not the deliberate policy of the Church to maintain a system of uneven distribution, although its loan policy may have been a contributory cause in the survival of the large estates which were established early in the colonial period. The officials of the *Juzgado* would almost certainly have maintained that they were operating an independent and legal fiscal policy and that the division of the land was a matter pertaining to the civil authorities alone. In fact, from the general viewpoint the lending activities of the Church did have some effect on land tenure. One economist has recently written that in Mexico credit was given to those who seemed to need it, but who in practice needed it least. Ecclesiastical credit could be as liberal as it was

---

[1] *Exposición del illmo. y venerable Cabildo de Puebla al Excelentísimo Sr. vice-presidente D. Anastasio Bustamante...*, 17 March 1830; *Colección eclesiástica mexicana*, IV, 77.

[2] These details are taken from an undated and unaddressed letter in AGN, PBN, leg. 27, exp. 84.

because it was never given without the additional security. The small farmer could not provide this security, but on the other hand the great landowners were able to do so, and hence they were the ones who obtained the credit.[1] In other words, clerical insistence on real estate as the only satisfactory security tended to perpetuate the existing landowners, whether good or bad, and thereby prevented the small, and presumably ambitious, farmer from obtaining credit with which to develop his land. The peasant and small farmer were condemned to poverty, for they could not improve their production without financial assistance, which in turn they could not obtain without first raising the value of their land by increased production. This criticism is sound in retrospect, but the clergy of the time would have rejected it on the grounds that no person or institution could be expected to lend money, especially belonging to other people, without a very secure guarantee to cover any possible loss, and that the only safe guarantee was real estate.

The effects of clerical investment in property are complicated and they have been generally misinterpreted, largely because of the sort of criticism first expounded in detail by Mora. His main error, and one that has been repeated by numerous subsequent authors, was to exaggerate the effects of the loan system operated by the Church. The general influence of this on property was not seriously detrimental to the sale, purchase, movement, and value of real estate. Indeed, the Church maintained that its lending activities were of great assistance to farmers and the development of rural economy. In 1830 the metropolitan chapter indicated a number of cases of this assistance. For example, any farmer who was unable to sell his crop, perhaps because the price was too low due to a surplus supply, was able to borrow money from pious funds and thereby purchase the seed he required for the next year's planting. Others, because of drought, an extreme frost, or some other accident, may have lost their crops and be on the verge of ruin. They could borrow money from the Church and continue to cultivate their land. Farmers could borrow money to buy livestock or to construct irrigation plants, and for any such project

[1] O. A. Hernández, *Esquema de la economía mexicana hasta antes de la revolución* (Mexico, 1961), p. 83.

there was no other source of capital except the Church.[1] As regards urban property, the Church maintained that its lending policy enabled people to buy their own houses, and in addition, by assuming a mortgage, the buyers were able to reserve their capital for more productive and beneficial use.[2]

It is difficult to refute such claims as these. The investment by the Church, however, did become a contributory cause of the lack of progress in agricultural development. But the mortgage debt owed by most farmers only became a burden because of a series of circumstances which the Church could not have foreseen and could not prevent. Few voices were raised in protest during the colonial period against the financial activities of the clergy and it was during these three centuries that the capital debt on the land accumulated to such an extent that it was unlikely that it could or ever would be repaid. The Church provided an essential service in the form of credit which no other institution was able to do.

Nevertheless, in the nineteenth century the Church found itself in a situation which was harmful to the country but for which it was not responsible. Each person who had borrowed money from the *Juzgado* or the regular orders had done so in the full knowledge that he was expected to pay interest charges on the debt, and, presumably, at the time of signing the contract most borrowers were confident of their ability to fulfil this obligation. However, because of the Church's lenient policy with regard to extensions and redemptions of loans, most of the capital remained invested for generations and successive owners were encumbered with the debt. The agricultural system set up in the colonial period whereby the owners of the land were rarely farmers and had little or no interest in the development of their estates led to a backward and unproductive agriculture. In spite of this borrowers in colonial times were able to make a sufficient income to enable them to pay the interest on their debts. But those who inherited these mortgages in the nineteenth century, and those who assumed new ones, found it increasingly difficult to do so, because the advances in methods of agricultural production, which might have enabled

[1] '*Exposición del cabildo de México...*'; *Colección eclesiástica mexicana*, IV, 62–3.
[2] *La Cruz*, 22 July 1858.

them to continue without hardship or difficulty to pay the interest or even redeem the capital, were to a large extent nullified by the numerous revolutions and wars which took place during the first forty years of independence. The interest charge became a hardship and often the only solution was to borrow further capital from the Church. This problem was realized by the liberals and in particular by Mora, who, in his zeal for reform, overstated his case and based many of his conclusions on incorrect information.

The Church was, therefore, in many respects a victim of circumstances beyond its control, and for which it was not responsible. No just criticism can be made of the way in which the ecclesiastical corporations, with perhaps the exception of the convents, managed their legally acquired wealth. The *Juzgado* was generous in the terms which it required of borrowers, even though this generosity caused the loss of a considerable amount of capital and revenue. Also, as is evident from the loan which was given to Guadalupe Victoria, at least some of the officials of the *Juzgado* were anxious to assist in the economic development of the country, but in this they were of necessity restricted by the amount and the nature of the funds at their disposal.

It was often alleged that the Church could have used its wealth in much more productive investments, particularly in projects which required large amounts of capital. The following questions were asked in 1855 in the newspaper *La Revolución*:

Do the clergy lend money to improve roads? No.
Do the clergy lend money for the development of mines? No.
Do the clergy lend money needed for the organization of industrial establishments? No.
Do the clergy lend money to the artisan so that he can open a workshop? No.
Do the clergy ever risk the most insignificant sum in enterprises which are useful to the country? No, no, and no.[1]

From the documentary evidence studied in connection with the many loans given by the *Juzgado* and the convents, the answer to all these questions is not entirely accurate, but the writer of 1855 was

[1] Cited in *La Cruz*, 8 November 1855.

to some extent justified in his criticism. The Church did contribute funds to certain public works but the *Juzgado* and the regular orders could not provide all the financial backing for the construction of new roads, firstly because there is no evidence that they were ever asked to do so, and secondly because the flow of revenue to the Church was continuous but small, and the demand for loans was so great and by so many individuals requiring small amounts that there was no opportunity to build up large reserves of capital. As in the example of the loan given to Lucas Alamán, the money was no sooner paid into the *Juzgado* than it was again lent to an individual borrower. Also, the nature of the revenue prevented the accumulation of large sums, for it must be remembered that the money used by the *Juzgado* and the regular orders was almost entirely committed to specific purposes, such as the *capellanías* and the pious works, and that it was the duty and function of the Church to invest the funds it received so as to yield a fixed income. The *Juzgado* could not retain the capitals of the *capellanías* in order to accumulate a large sum, which could then be invested in the construction of a new factory or a new road, for the interest on each foundation had to be paid immediately and continuously. Hence the money had to be invested quickly and above all safely, which of course resulted in the use of real estate as the only satisfactory security. The Church could not be expected to speculate with the money entrusted to it by individual citizens. The only revenue which the Church could have used in speculative ventures came from the tithes, but as we have seen, these were virtually abolished in 1833. The Church, therefore, lent money in small sums to the farmer, merchant, and industrialist, and in this way contributed to the economic development.

There are some examples to show that the Church was willing to invest in large-scale enterprises. For example, the General Mining Fund, established in 1777 to promote the development of mines, was well supported by the clerical corporations. In a list of creditors to the fund drawn up in 1849, not only the *Juzgado*, but also many convents and parishes, were included.[1] Also there is

---

[1] *Exposición que los acreedores al fondo dotal de minería elevan a la Augusta Cámara de Diputados en defensa de sus derechos* (Mexico, 1849).

evidence to indicate that the Church was not unwilling to invest in the construction of roads. In 1803 the merchant guild of Vera Cruz was instructed by the Viceroy to build a road from Vera Cruz to Perote to facilitate the inland traffic. The guild found that it was unable to finance the project alone and it sought the help of investors. The income from the road toll was to be used as security for the loans, which received 5 per cent interest. By 1849 the government proposed that the right to the toll income should be taken from the investors, who immediately appealed against this decision. Among the appealing creditors were the convents of San Lorenzo and Santa Catalina de Sena, the province of Santiago de Predicadores de Mexico, the congregation of Nuestra Señora de Balvanera, and the brotherhood of Dulce Nombre de Jesús.[1]

In fact the main deficiency in the loan system operated by the *Juzgado* and the other corporations was that no check or supervision was kept on the way in which the money was used by the borrowers. Most of the latter gave no specific reason for wanting a loan and there was no way of ensuring that the capital was employed in a productive manner, beneficial to the general economic progress of the nation. The Church, as the sole institution in possession of and able to invest capital, was to some extent responsible for utilizing its funds to the best advantage from the point of view of the country as a whole. In fact the clergy did not accept this wide responsibility, and insisted that their only duty was to the real owners of the funds, namely the founders of the many benefices and those who endowed pious works. The *Juzgado* was not really concerned with what happened to its money once it had left the coffers, so long as the security remained adequate and the interest was paid. Consequently, clerical insistence on the economic benefits derived from their loan system was based purely on the assumption that the borrowers made good use of the funds which they acquired, and such benefits, as far as the Church was concerned, were essentially a chance result of, rather than the main purpose of, the fiscal policy. There were,

---

[1] *Exposición dirigida al congreso general por la Comisión de acreedores al camino de Perote a Veracruz pidiendo no se comprendan en las medidas propuestas por la Comisión de Crédito Público de la Cámara de Diputados, las hipotecas del peage y la avería que especialmente están consignadas a los mismos acreedores* (Mexico, 1849).

of course, exceptions to this and particularly the Fiscal Advisers to the *Juzgado* seem to have been acutely conscious of the need to put clerical riches to productive use.

Generally speaking the Church considered itself the trustee of much of its wealth, and that its main duty was to carry out the wishes of those who had entrusted it with their goods. The *Juzgado* and the regular orders were rarely free to dispose of their revenue as they wished. They had to ensure that the capital fund yielded the required interest and as far as possible was safely invested. Finally, although the fiscal activities of the clergy may in some respects have hindered the economic development of the country, both Mora and subsequent liberals neglected the fact that the Church was only able to pursue its investment policy because of public demand for financial assistance. It is difficult to imagine how any alternative credit system could have operated with greater success in the circumstances of the times or with any difference in the eventual results.

# CHAPTER 5

# THE 'JUZGADO' AND THE STATE

In comparison with other clerical corporations such as the convents and monasteries, the position of the *Juzgado* within independent Mexico was relatively secure and no direct attempt at abolition was made even when the liberals were in full control of the national government. This was mainly due to the nature of the institution and its activities for, although a unit within the corporate body of the Church, the *Juzgado* was in most respects a secular organization. Its employees, with the important exception of the Judge, were rarely ordained members of the Church, and its daily business was almost exclusively concerned, either directly or indirectly, with commercial and financial matters. Furthermore, even though its capital and revenue were considered to be sacred funds, the Fiscal rightly pointed out in 1813 that the many *capellanías* managed by the officials were not really ecclesiastical benefices, but were rather trust funds which the wealthy had established for the use of their descendants.[1] Hence the Church as a whole in fact received little financial return from the *capellanías*, for the only obligation laid upon the recipient, to whom the net income was paid, was to say a certain number of masses each year for the soul of his benefactor. The *capellanes* had to be ordained but they were not required to perform any religious or spiritual exercise which brought material benefit to the Church. In many cases they became clerics only in order to qualify for a benefice. In this respect, therefore, the *Juzgado* was essentially an administrative organization charged with managing capital which belonged to the lay population, and with providing an income to persons who were often clerics in nothing but name.

From the viewpoint of the State, the way in which the *Juzgado* employed its wealth determined governmental action. The distribution of clerical funds by means of personal loans to the land-

---

[1] Fiscal to Archbishop, 2 December 1813, AGN, PBN, leg. 330, exp. 29.

owners, farmers, and businessmen of the country meant that it was virtually impossible to retrieve the money without antagonizing the most powerful and influential sector of society. As a result of the general economic situation and the great scarcity of capital which arose after independence, few of those who negotiated loans were able or willing to redeem the principal at the end of the first or subsequent contracted terms. They were unable to do so regardless of whether redemption was demanded by either the Church or the State. Consequently, unlike the real estate assets owned by the regular orders, the invested capital of the *Juzgado* was secure from confiscation, for it was in the possession of the lay population. This fact was gradually realized by successive independence governments and with the advent to power of the Juárez administration it was clear that the only effective means whereby any government could gain possession of these pious funds was to transfer the ownership and trusteeship of them to the State. Even such a measure as this could achieve only a limited success in that the interest would be paid to the nation, whereas the principals would mostly have to remain in the hands of the impecunious borrowers, at least until there had been a general improvement in the prosperity of the property-owning classes. The law of nationalization of clerical goods, issued on 12 July 1859, was the first major attempt since independence to dispossess the *Juzgado* of its funds. In spite of the political and military dominance of Juárez at this time, the measure achieved little success, and relatively few of the loans were retrieved.[1]

Until the liberal victory and subsequent defeat of the conservative and pro-clerical forces, both national and State governments, through their own weakness, had been limited to a policy which merely attempted to control the revenue and activities of the *Juzgado* or else to reduce them by means of taxation. By and large this policy failed and the fact that it did so provides a significant indication of the change in the relative strength of both the Church and the State once the colonial regime had ended. On

---

[1] The government replaced the ecclesiastical corporations as creditor and established rules for the redemption of mortgages formerly held by the Church. In spite of the easy terms which were allowed, disputes over repayment of the mortgages lasted until well into the Díaz regime. For this information I am indebted to Professor R. J. Knowlton.

the one hand the power of the civil authority was weakened, with the result that the position of the Church was strengthened. Throughout the colonial period the Church had acknowledged the supreme authority of the Spanish Crown, and if the latter ordered the appropriation or confiscation of clerical goods the clergy rarely challenged the right of the monarch to implement such measures, although objections might be raised on other grounds. Indeed, during the war of independence the clergy actively supported decrees against clerical goods. In 1815 Dr Osores, who was later to be head of the *Juzgado*, said that the State, in the person of the monarch, was perfectly entitled to use ecclesiastical wealth in cases of national emergency. This attitude soon changed. In 1847 the same Dr Osores expressed the opposite view and declared that Church goods were sacred and inalienable, regardless of the emergency situation which had arisen as a result of the war with America.[1] After independence, the Church refused to accept that the State had any legal jurisdiction or power over clerical wealth and the clergy resisted any proposed confiscation.[2] Such was the relative strength of the Church that no civil government until that of Juárez had sufficient power to implement any measure adversely affecting the funds of the *Juzgado* and other corporations.

This had not been the case during the colonial regime, when the central authority of the monarch was absolute and the administrative organization of the colony was more comprehensive and efficient. This was clearly illustrated at the beginning of the nineteenth century when the laws of consolidation were introduced. One of the main difficulties involved in confiscating the capitals of benefices and pious works was to acquire the details

---

[1] This change of view was noted by an anonymous writer who, in a letter to the *Diario Oficial* published on 22 January 1847, pointed out that Dr Osores had in 1815 written and proved with references to both civil and canon law that if the nation was in danger it was quite legal to appropriate even the most sacred of goods. The writer continues with details of the clerical moneys which Dr Osores himself had ordered should be given to the royalists and he verifies his allegations by sending a copy of the exposition and decree which authorized the confiscation.

[2] Clerical views on the inalienability of Church wealth were widely disseminated in the many representations which greeted almost every anti-clerical law; for some of these representations see *Colección eclesiástica mexicana*, IV.

of the foundations and of those persons who had borrowed the funds. Several post-independence governments tried to gather this information but they were unsuccessful, first because the Church would not co-operate and provide its records for inspection, and secondly because the notarial records, in which details of every loan contract were in theory kept, proved to be in such disorder that they were virtually useless.[1] These problems did not exist in the tightly controlled colonial administrative system.

It was on 26 December 1804 that a royal decree ordered the implementation of the laws of consolidation. These laws entailed the first direct attack on the funds of the *Juzgado*, for they required that the invested capital of the Church should be withdrawn from circulation and placed at the disposal of the viceregal officials. The Crown was to pay interest at the rate of 3 per cent per annum on the total amount appropriated. There was opposition from the Church, but unlike the reaction to similar measures introduced in the independent nation, this was not based on their legality or on the right of the monarch to issue them, but on the disastrous effects which their execution would have on agriculture and the economy in general. Bishop Abad y Queipo estimated in 1805 that ecclesiastical funds comprised two-thirds of the active capital in circulation in the colony, and that if it was withdrawn agriculture, commerce, and mining would be ruined. Nevertheless, in spite of the obvious arguments against the measure, the financial position of the monarch was so desperate that the laws were carried out. Ecclesiastical co-operation in the task of assessing the capitals that were to be withdrawn was not required. Two circulars were issued by the Viceroy on 28 August and 10 September 1805, in which all notaries and scribes were ordered to present lists of every clerical benefice or foundation which they had drawn up or witnessed during the previous few years. On this occasion the notaries seem to have had no hesitation or difficulty in supplying

---

[1] Almost every Minister of Justice sought to compile statistics of the various personnel and funds of the Church. Until 1833 they achieved some cooperation from the clergy and many detailed accounts are to be found in the annual reports of the Ministry. After the attempted liberal reform of 1833–4, however, the Church was unwilling to disclose information about its wealth and several efforts to persuade the *Juzgado* to give details of *capellanías* met with no success.

the requested information. The lists which they submitted, some of which date back to 1789, enabled the royal officials to trace each capital and demand its repayment.[1] When similar information was requested after 1821 it proved impossible to obtain.

The laws of consolidation were of great significance, for they provided a precedent on which subsequent governments were able to assess the results of any measures against the invested funds of the *Juzgado*. The effects on agriculture seem to have been as Abad y Queipo predicted. In 1818 a writer discussed the decline which had taken place in agricultural production and he blamed this in part on the fact that many farmers had been forced to raise substantial amounts of capital to redeem their mortgages in accordance with the royal decrees. Secondly, he felt that the withdrawal of the ecclesiastical capital had deprived the farmer of the credit facilities which he required, particularly as a result of the independence war.[2] Certainly, in comparison with the eighteenth century, the *Juzgado* after 1821 had much less capital to distribute, and inevitably loans were of smaller amounts and under more stringent terms, for example the invariable need to have real estate as security. Not only did the borrowers suffer, but also the beneficiaries of the confiscated capital, that is the *capellanes*. In 1825 the Minister of Justice emphasized that the shortage of clergy at that time was partly caused by the destruction of so many benefices of which the principal had been paid into the royal coffers.[3] Furthermore, many pious works, the income of which had been devoted to charitable institutions, schools, and hospitals, were also ruined. Clearly, a great many people were affected either directly or indirectly by any attack on the *Juzgado*'s funds, and to any independence government which needed political support and popularity a measure similar to that of the consolidation was dangerous, even if desirable on financial and economic grounds.

---

[1] Some of these lists are in AGN, PBN, leg. 1767, exp. 1.

[2] J. M. Quirós, *Memoria de estatuto. Causas de que ha procedido que la agricultura, industria y minería de Nueva España no hayan adquirido el gran fomento de que son susceptibles. Medidas que contribuirán a que se restablezcan de la ruina que les ha ocasionado la insurección de sus provincias* (Mexico, 1818), pp 2–3.

[3] *Memoria de Justicia* (1825) p. 19.

The amount involved in this 'terrible attack or rather plunder', as it was called in 1825, has not yet been firmly established.[1] There are numerous calculations of the total confiscated throughout the country which is generally estimated at a little over ten million pesos, but there are few which concern the archbishopric.[2] Ecclesiastical records have retained many of the accounts which were made in the diocese at the time of the laws being carried out; for example, one is entitled *List of the Principals paid into the 'Real Caja de Consolidación'*.[3] According to this account, from 6 September 1805 to 20 October 1806 the sum of 1,518,626 pesos was paid to the royal officials. Further amounts were paid totalling 339,798 pesos but no date is given, although as they follow on from the earlier entries it seems likely that they were handed over in 1807. If this is so then the total given in 1805, 1806, and 1807 amounted to 1,858,424 pesos. Another account shows that in 1808 671,433 pesos were collected and paid.[4] Thus the total capital withdrawn from circulation in the archbishopric amounted to 2,529,857 pesos, most of which was taken from the funds of the *Juzgado*.[5]

This massive confiscation of clerical capital was motivated by the financial needs of the Spanish monarch, for as long as the royal treasury was not completely empty no serious attempt had previously been made to limit or deprive the *Juzgado* and other corporations of this particular part of their wealth. Because of the separation from Spain, however, there was little or no possibility of the money ever being repaid to the Church. Nevertheless, the *Juzgado* and the convents carefully guarded the credits which they were given in exchange for their funds and in their annual accounts long and comprehensive details were kept of the amounts

---

[1] *Ibid.*

[2] For example, see Alamán, *Historia de México*, I, 140; N. de Zamacois, *Historia de México* (Barcelona, 1787–88), vol. XV, p. 284.

[3] This account is in AGN, PBN, leg. 958, exp. 37.

[4] This account is in the form of a book and is in AGN, PBN, leg. 1745, exp. 1. It is entitled *Cargo de México*. In the same expediente there is a similar volume for each of the other dioceses.

[5] This total can be verified by later statements, for example in 1826 the Chief Notary of the *Juzgado* calculated that almost two and a half millions had been paid into consolidation; Atilano Sánchez, unaddressed, 23 December 1826, AGN, *Justicia Eclesiástica*, vol. 96, fol. 166.

owed and the interest due.¹ There was some reason for this care. In the first place, until the formal recognition of independence, there was always the possibility that Spain might reconquer her former colony, although this was clearly remote. Secondly, there was some financial speculation in these credits, especially as the Church came to realize that they would never be fully redeemed. As early as 1819, even before the final break from Spain, the metropolitan prelate sold a consolidation credit with a face value of 100,000 pesos for only 40,000, and some years later the convent of La Encarnación sold credits to the value of 700,000 pesos for only 60,000. Individual *capellanes*, who in many cases must have been deprived of their only source of income as a result of the consolidation laws, were allowed to sell their own claims to any buyer they could find.² Again in 1830 the diocese sold 800,000 pesos worth of consolidation credits for a very low price, and shortly afterwards one José Rojas asked if he could buy a similar amount.³ The Fiscal, in his report on the proposal, pointed out that there was virtually no chance of the bonds ever being redeemed.

This opinion of the Fiscal was not shared by the financial speculators. The credits were in such demand because the independence governments had assumed the nation's standing internal debt in 1821, which included the consolidation funds. In later years the civil authorities often accepted this type of credit in part payment of taxes or forced loans. It was not therefore complete foolishness on the part of the speculators to try to acquire them. Many did so. An interesting case occurred in 1848 at a time when the Church was desperately trying to raise large amounts of capital to be used in redeeming bills sold by the government. On 5 October 1848 the representatives of the English firm of Manning and Makintosh wrote to the head of the archdiocese to inquire if the Church was prepared to sell to them any interest-yielding credits which the ecclesiastical corporations held against the pre-independence government. They proposed to buy such credits to

---

¹ There is a copy of one of the credits in AGN, PBN, leg. 1760, exp. 1.
² These details are taken from a letter from the Fiscal to the Judge, 10 June 1839, AGN, PBN, leg. 1035, exp. 1.
³ J. Rojas to chapter, undated, 1830, AGN, PBN, leg. 967, exp. 13.

the value of one million pesos and they offered to pay 10 per cent of their face value. On the next day clerical and company officials met and agreed to the sale under the following terms: the Church would sell credits, recognized by the government, to the value of 1,209,657 pesos, which would be bought by the firm of Manning and Makintosh for 8 per cent of their face value; these would be paid for by the latter as follows, 20,000 pesos within one month, a further 20,000 within the first year at the rate of 1666 pesos per month, and the remainder of the purchase price, (56,772 pesos) over a period of five years; the total was to bear interest at the rate of 6 per cent. The value of the credits which were bought by Manning and Makintosh was later raised to 1,548,100 pesos. The deal proved reasonably satisfactory to the Church and by 1851 the amount yielded was 123,848 pesos, of which 72,000 had been paid. Some of the remaining debt of the English firm was transferred to meet the demands of other creditors, for example Agustín Prado held 83,000 pesos worth of notes from two government loans and the Church was responsible for their redemption. An agreement was reached with him on 31 October 1848 by which the Church had to pay 35,000 pesos in cash, but the remainder of the debt was settled by transferring to the creditor some of the claims which were held against Manning and Makintosh.[1]

The credits which were used in this and other similar negotiations were mainly those consolidation bonds which the *Juzgado* and other corporations still held, and any profit made by the Church was distributed to the owners or trustees of the benefices which had been confiscated. The *Juzgado*, of course, received most of the money, although inevitably it regained only a very small part of the total confiscated.

The laws of consolidation, therefore, had considerable long-term effects. Post-independence governments were unable or unwilling to implement similar measures because of the reasons already mentioned, namely, the political effects on the generally middle and upper class borrowers, and the inability of the

[1] These details are taken from *Memoria secreta*, AGN, PBN, leg. 81, exp. 1. See also my article on 'Church-State Financial Negotiations...', *Revista de Historia de América*.

borrowers to redeem their loans in view of the widespread poverty and lack of economic development, which in themselves were partly the result of the great scarcity of capital. Nevertheless, the intervention of the clergy in the political sphere, the supposed economic effects of the *Juzgado*'s investment policy as expounded by the liberals, and the desperate financial position of the national government, meant that some action would be taken against the institution. Confiscation similar to that of the consolidation was impossible and hence a less radical and far reaching measure had to be devised.

Such a measure originated in the State Congress of Mexico in 1833. On 7 May of that year the Congress, meeting at Toluca, which was the capital of the State, issued the following decree:

The Government will effect, as quickly as possible, the transfer to this City, Seat of the Supreme Powers, those foundations of the *Juzgado de Testamentos, Capellanías y Obras Pías*, which are mortgaged on properties within the State.[1]

The next day an official was appointed to implement this transfer. On 17 May the chief financial adviser to the diocese advised the ruling chapter to protest at once and to appoint a commission whose terms of reference would be to indicate the harmful and detrimental effects which the proposed transfer would cause. On receipt of this advice the chapter ordered that the opinions of the Judge and his advisers should be sought. On 28 May the official named by the government to execute the decree wrote to the diocesan secretary to complain about the delay and the fact that the Judge had not yet presented his report on the matter. Two days later the Fiscal reported his opinions, and needless to say he opposed the measure. He made a number of observations and argued that there was no need to establish what would in effect be a second *Juzgado*. The one in existence was already greatly restricted in its activities in that it could only sue for debt in the civil courts and had no jurisdiction over testamentary cases. Furthermore, the metropolitan Church was under no obligation

---

[1] A copy of this decree and the correspondence pertaining to it are in AGN, PBN, leg. 364, exp. 6.

to invest its funds within the state of Mexico, and had in fact given many loans to people residing in distant parts of the country. In any case, the majority of the patrons and *capellanes* of benefices, the funds of which were invested in the State, already lived elsewhere and it would be a simple matter for the *Juzgado* to transfer the mortgages once the term of the contracts had expired. The Fiscal then made a most unexpected admission. The State authorities had argued that the capitals invested in the territory in fact belonged to the State, which ought therefore to have some control over them. In response to this the Fiscal admitted that Church goods in a sense were the property of the nation, but rejected the idea that they could belong to any one part or region. Such an admission was directly contrary to official Church policy which constantly refused to accept that the nation had any legal rights over ecclesiastical wealth. Finally, the Fiscal pointed out that if the principle of establishing a *Juzgado* wherever funds were invested was adopted, this would mean the creation of dozens of new offices, for ecclesiastical capital was distributed in almost every state. Clearly, he argued, such duplication was unnecessary, particularly in view of the now much reduced activities of the *Juzgado*.[1]

This lengthy and logical report from the Fiscal and the inevitable opposition of the Church were sufficient to delay any action by the State authorities. Eventually, more than a year later, the law was officially revoked on 5 November 1834. The State Congress had tried unsuccessfully to gain a limited control over the *Juzgado*.[2] The national governments adopted different methods but with virtually the same result, partly because every attempt at control or restriction was met with an outcry of protest by those most affected, that is, the property-owning borrowers. These

---

[1] Fiscal to Judge, 30 May 1833, *ibid.*

[2] Some years earlier the State Congress of Querétaro tried to introduce a similar restrictive measure. A committee of deputies proposed that the Judge be ordered not to remove any capital already invested in the State. If a loan was redeemed, the money had to be reinvested within the State boundaries. The Fiscal rejected the proposal on the grounds that it represented an attack on the laws of property and the right of the individual to place his funds wherever he wished. He pointed out also that if every state adopted the same attitude, Querétaro would get very few new investments. The documents concerning this are in AGN, PBN, leg. 429, exp. 41.

measures, taken usually on a national scale, consisted of a series of laws designed to restrict the activities and fiscal autonomy of the *Juzgado* and to achieve for the government some limited supervision over the use of clerical funds. The first law appeared on 20 November 1833, when the regular orders were forbidden to sell property or to transfer capital.[1] Just over a month later any movement of property or capital was forbidden.[2] Similar restrictive laws were issued on 24 January and 9 July 1834.[3] Then the pro-clerical centralist administration of Santa Anna came to power and on 25 May 1835 these previous decrees were repealed and the ecclesiastical corporations were again free to dispose of their possessions.[4]

These early laws only marginally affected the *Juzgado* in so far as some of the benefices belonging to the regular orders were managed by the Judge and his officials, but they did provide an example which was soon followed. On 4 August 1838 the regular orders were again forbidden to sell any of their goods without having previously obtained the permission of the government to do so.[5] Then on 27 June 1842 a circular was issued by the Minister of Justice in which he complained that this previous decree was not being observed. All notaries were warned not to execute any sale or disposal of clerical possessions unless official consent had been received. Furthermore, on this occasion a new and significant addition was introduced, that is the redemption of invested capital was now restricted.[6] A few months later, on 3 February 1843, another circular extended these restrictions to cover all ecclesiastical institutions including the *Juzgado*.[7] This caused some confusion and the Fiscal made several representations against this encroachment on clerical authority.[8] As a result of these protests the Minister stated that the *Juzgado* and other corporations could continue to redeem and invest capital without prior permission, but they were not allowed to sell property without official approval.[9]

[1] Dublán y Lozano, II, 635.  [2] Law of 24 December 1833, *ibid.* II, 656.
[3] Dublán y Lozano, II, 668–9, 710.  [4] *Ibid.* III, 53.
[5] *Ibid.* III, 538–9.  [6] *Ibid.* IV, 224.
[7] *Ibid.* IV, 363.
[8] One of these is in AGN, *Justicia Eclesiástica*, vol. 123, fols. 326–34.
[9] Circular of Minister of Justice, 1 July 1843, Dublán y Lozano, IV, 473.

The confusion over the exact meaning of these various decrees persisted. In 1845 the convent of Santa Inés received permission from the government to redeem the sum of 3,000 pesos provided that it was immediately reinvested. The Archbishop decided to consult his advisers on whether it was still necessary to seek permission for the redemption of capital. José María Barrientos reported that permission was only required for the sale of property or capital, but that because of ignorance of the law a number of public notaries were still refusing to authorize redemptions or transfers of loans without official permission to do so. He suggested that the prelate should ask the Minister for yet another explanatory circular on the matter.[1] This was eventually done and the Minister replied that no permission was needed.[2] Some notaries still continued in ignorance of the law, for some two months later the Judge complained to the Minister that the Mortgage Office had refused to acknowledge the cancellation of a mortgage because the redemption had been made without the approval of the civil authorities.[3] The Minister replied that such permission was not required.

These laws were again revoked by Santa Anna on 29 March 1847, but it was soon found necessary to reintroduce similar ones, for the Church was finding it increasingly difficult to raise the large sums needed to finance the several loans which it had agreed to make to the government. The *Juzgado* in particular was in a difficult position, for it was asked on several occasions to make substantial contributions to the loans. It had no reserves of capital and all its funds were entailed in mortgages that had already been given. The Church authorities eventually recognized this fact but in the meantime the Judge faced the problem of raising funds quickly. The only solution was to demand from borrowers the redemption of their loans. One example of this occurred in 1847, when the Legal Adviser was ordered to insist that a mortgage should be redeemed because of the *Juzgado*'s obligation to contribute to the governmental loans.[4] The borrowers, of course,

[1] J. M. Barrientos to Archbishop, 11 March 1845, AGN, PBN, leg. 534, exp. unmarked.
[2] Ruiz de Tejada to Archbishop, 2 April 1845, AGN, PBN, leg. 534, exp. unmarked (entitled *Solicitudes sin proveer*).
[3] Judge to Minister of Justice, 19 June 1845, AGN, PBN, leg. 284, exp. 6.
[4] Legal Adviser to Judge, 2 July 1847, AGN, PBN, leg. 582, exp. unmarked.

objected to this treatment and the government was, in effect, obliged to introduce a new restriction forbidding the Judge to take such action. The new law dated 17 May 1847 included other measures which represented a direct attack on the *Juzgado*'s funds. Article two stipulated that those properties which had been completely destroyed as a result of the war with America were relieved of any mortgages which were attached to them. The owners of those properties which had been partly damaged were to be given an appropriate reduction in the amount of their mortgages. Article three stated that as long as the war lasted the owners of rural properties which were damaged were to be allowed a reduction in their interest payments.[1] The reaction of the Church was immediately hostile and the attitude adopted was the same as that in 1821, when the Church refused to agree to any reduction in capital or interest debts because of the independence war. A strongly worded representation was quickly sent to the Minister of *Hacienda*, and this proved remarkably effective for the law was revoked, just over a fortnight after its issue, on 5 June 1847.

The Church appreciated the position of the government and its fear of public reaction and discontent if the clerical officials began to demand the redemption of all invested capital. Consequently, for once a compromise solution was reached whereby the clergy acceded to the government's wishes but at the same time retained control in their own hands. The head of the see issued a circular to all administrators and managers of ecclesiastical funds in which he ordered that no capitals were to be forcibly redeemed without his own prior written permission, which would only be given in cases of extreme need, and only when the money was specifically required to meet the monthly payments to the government.[2] Then on 14 July 1847 the Minister of Justice officially acknowledged that the ecclesiastical corporations had to be allowed to raise capital. The only condition attached to this was that the government should be kept informed of any sales.[3]

[1] Dublán y Lozano, v, 274.
[2] *Circular of* Vicario Capitular, 7 June 1847, AGN, *Justicia Eclesiástica*, vol. 159, fol. 380.
[3] Dublán y Lozano, v, 292.

Nevertheless, in spite of the above the civil officials were still resolved to maintain some supervision over the fiscal activities of the clergy. Hence only three days after the previous statement was issued, another circular was distributed in which the Minister requested that within eight days all scribes and notaries should present an account of every sale of urban or rural property, every redemption of a mortgage, and every new loan which had been made by the Church.[1] Although the Minister received some replies from other states, the Municipality of Mexico City said that it could not supply the requested information because of the numbers and confusion of the contracts involved.[2] The government could find no means, therefore, of keeping an accurate check on the movement of clerical goods.

Although the loans which the clergy had agreed to make to the government were mostly agreed upon in 1847, the effects of these were still being felt almost two years later when the Church was engaged in cashing the short-term treasury notes that had been sold. Even after the immediate financial crisis had passed the ecclesiastical corporations were still having to raise large sums of money, and some of them were doing this by calling in loans. The state congress now intervened and decreed on 3 January 1849 that the Church was not to demand the redemption of invested capital.[3] The *Vicario Capitular* decided to appeal against the law but first sought the opinion of one of his advisers, Dr Joaquín Román. The latter advised that the law should not be obeyed on the grounds that it had been issued by a single state and therefore only applied to that part of the diocese which lay within the jurisdiction of the State authorities. Hence it was impossible to implement. Furthermore, he deplored such anti-clerical measures and indicated at length the great effort which the Church had made to help the government. He wrote:

...two million pesos have already been handed over, not counting the loss of many capitals; many properties, both rural and urban, have been sacrificed and rarely has their sale yielded more than two-thirds of the

---

[1] Circular of Minister of Justice, 17 July 1847, AGN, *Justicia Eclesiástica*, vol. 48, fol. 183.
[2] Lic. Cástulo Barreda to Minister of Justice, 22 July 1847, *ibid.* fol. 272.
[3] A copy of this decree is in AGN, *Justicia Eclesiástica*, vol. 165, fol. 39.

true value; the circular issued by the *Vicario Capitular* has been faithfully observed and invested funds have not been redeemed in order to pay governmental loans, but only in those cases where interest was not being paid, or the security was no longer adequate.[1]

Acting on this advice, protests were made to the National Government with the result that on 23 April 1849 the President officially revoked the State decree.[2]

These many laws intended to restrict the sale and movement of clerical goods are a clear indication that the Church was constantly engaged in a variety of fiscal activities. The *Juzgado* had sold most of its houses by 1845 and the regular orders had sold many others. There had also been considerable movement of capital and investments. The exact reasons for this are not clear, particularly with regard to the sale of property. At first it would appear that it was undertaken because most of the houses were in poor condition and the rent collected did not provide an adequate return on capital. However, there is evidence to suggest that a more subtle policy was being pursued. Throughout the colonial period the ecclesiastical corporations, and in particular the regular orders, were allowed to gain possession of extensive amounts of property, and in the early years of the nineteenth century their policy of acquiring direct ownership of real estate was to some extent continued. In 1813 the prioress of the convent of Santa Teresa wrote to the Archbishop concerning a house which was for sale in the capital. She pointed out the excellent condition of the property and implied that the price of 13,500 pesos was by no means high. She continued with details of the rental income and asked permission to purchase. This was granted some days later.[3]

The coming of independence saw a change in this policy of accumulation and many of the convents and other institutions, including the *Juzgado*, began to sell property on a considerable scale. There were several reasons for this change. In the first place, as has already been indicated, the financial resources of the civil governments after independence were extremely limited and

---

[1] Report of J. Román, 25 January 1849, AGN, PBN, leg. 200, exp. unmarked.
[2] The order for repeal is in AGN, *Justicia Eclesiástica*, vol. 165, fol. 55.
[3] The documents concerning this are in AGN, PBN, leg. 412, exp. 2.

various administrations found themselves obliged to seek revenue from the wealth of the Church. Loans were forced upon or sometimes offered by the clergy. The burden of these fell largely on those corporations within the Church which owned property, for real estate was an asset which could be sold relatively quickly. The fact that a considerable number of houses within the capital city were released in an already depressed real estate market inevitably resulted in low prices. The clergy found themselves having to accept a price that was considerably lower than the true value. For example, in 1853 the Congregation of San Felipe Neri decided to sell some houses for which they were offered only two-thirds of the valuation price.[1] They accepted this offer and again two years later another house, valued at 2,889 pesos, was sold to Manuel Prieto for 1,926 pesos, which was the highest offer received.[2]

A number of these sales of property were clearly necessary for financial reasons, but there are indications that political motives were also partly responsible as a result of the increasingly strong attack on clerical goods. The confiscatory measures advocated by the liberals brought the ecclesiastical corporations to the conclusion that their capital wealth would be more secure if invested in the form of mortgages. Invested capital had proved in the case of the consolidation to be difficult to confiscate and it was clear that only an extremely strong civil administration could afford to take the obvious political risks involved in forcing people to redeem loans that had often been borrowed by their family several generations earlier. Certainly from the clerical point of view it was no longer advisable to keep all assets in the easily confiscated form of property. This radical change in fiscal policy was clearly stated by the provincial of Carmen, who maintained that it was undoubtedly sounder business to invest money than to buy real estate. The provincial wrote in 1834 that in certain times it was indeed better to own property, but that in the present circumstances it was more advisable to convert one's real estate holdings into investment capital, and that self-interest alone would advocate such a policy.[3]

[1] See AGN, PBN, leg. 164 exp. 10.    [2] *Ibid.* leg. 164, exp. unmarked.
[3] *Exposición del Provincial del Carmen* (Mexico, 1834), p. 9.

This idea was not in fact new, for as early as 1787 the administrator of the convent of Balvanera had suggested to the prelate that all the houses owned by the convent should be sold and that the new owners should recognize the purchase price in a contract that would be perpetual, the owner paying 5 per cent interest calculated on the capital value of the house. The reasons for this proposal were simply that by relinquishing ownership the convent would avoid the expense of repairs and the problems of bad tenants.[1] The document from which this information is taken gives no indication as to the result of the suggestion, but there is no doubt that it was rejected because the convent continued to own a number of houses after 1787.

It seems likely that the *Juzgado*'s sale of its property was based on the same fiscal policy being followed by the regular orders. The clergy seem to have increased their sale of real estate whenever pressure for clerical reform began to build up. The civil governments were not, of course, slow to realize this fact and they were well aware of the difficulties involved in retrieving mortgage funds. The laws that have been outlined were designed in most instances to stop the changeover from property to invested capital, but they failed because the government had to allow the Church to raise funds if the clergy were to meet the agreed and very necessary loans. The position of the *Juzgado* was from the beginning more secure than that of the regular orders. The Church itself recognized that its income and capital should not be confiscated or even drawn upon for any purpose other than that laid down in the terms of the foundations to which all funds belonged. This fact was illustrated in connection with the loan which the clergy in the archdiocese agreed to make to the government in December 1846. The amount involved was 850,000 pesos, and in order to raise this clerical officials drew up an account of the disposable income and capital of every ecclesiastical institution within the diocese, and on the basis of these figures a certain sum was allocated to each corporation. The *Juzgado* was originally asked to pay 31,500 but because all of its capital was invested, and therefore not quickly realizable, and because its

[1] Juan Cordero de Gijón to Archbishop, 5 July 1787, AGN, PBN, leg. 145, exp. 47.

funds were only held in trust by the Church, it was excused payment of the whole amount.[1]

The fact that the Judge had disposed of most of the real estate also proved fortunate, for in January 1847 the government of Gómez Farías ordered the appropriation of clerical property to the value of fifteen million pesos, one-third of which was to be taken from the archbishopric. Government officials began to draw up lists of houses which were to be confiscated and they did not hesitate to include the *Juzgado*. Among the records of the latter there is an account dated 8 February 1847 and entitled: 'Properties belonging to the *Juzgado de Capellanías* which the commissioner designated by the government of the Federal District, will occupy in the name of the Supreme Government.' This list was made out by an official of the Ministry of *Hacienda* and contained a total of fourteen properties.[2] Subsequent events prevented the implementation of the general law of confiscation and the *Juzgado* was not forced to part with its few remaining houses.

The material possessions of the Church were not only the object of confiscations and attempts at control or restriction, but were also subjected to heavy taxation. The amortization tax established by the Spanish monarch in 1789 was continued after independence. This required that 15 per cent of the value of any real estate or capital acquired by the Church after 1798 should be paid as a tax to the State, and the law was confirmed in 1842 by Santa Anna.[3] It has been estimated that by 1858 the revenue from this tax alone had yielded more than three-quarters of a million pesos.[4] Also, the Church was subject to the *alcabala* tax and, after independence, to the innumerable property taxes that were levied almost yearly between 1835 and 1849. The latter were particularly onerous to the *Juzgado*, for the houseowner whose property was mortgaged was allowed to deduct a certain amount of the tax from the interest payments on the mortgage debt. Some of these taxes were temporary, that is imposed only once, for example, those decreed on the following dates: 21 November 1835, 8 June

[1] These facts are taken from *Memoria secreta*, AGN, PBN, leg. 81, exp. 1.
[2] This list is in AGN, PBN, leg. 734, exp. 24.
[3] Dublán y Lozano, IV, 254.      [4] *La Cruz*, 22 July 1858.

1838, 21 August 1844, 2 October 1846, and 30 December 1846. As the Church was the largest owner of real estate in the country, it bore the heaviest burden of these taxes, some of which were on the capital value of rural or urban properties and some on rents. Other similar contributions were made annual, for example that of 30 June 1836, which amounted to a sum of two pesos in every thousand of the capital value of urban property.[1] This was followed on 5 July of the same year by a similar tax of three pesos in every thousand on rural property, and on 11 March 1841 this higher rate was extended to urban property.[2] A variety of other levies was introduced from which the clergy were not excused, for example, a tax on salaries, personal contributions, and a tax on business establishments, including the tithe collection districts.

Taxation, therefore, was probably the most fruitful of the numerous attempts by the State to gain possession of clerical wealth. The confiscatory measures that were proposed and even decreed yielded little revenue, for until 1856 the Church was almost invariably successful in defending its goods. Both liberal and conservative administrations found themselves powerless to impose any major appropriation, and they had to be content with loans and occasional minor confiscations which were of little interest or value to the Church as a whole. The attempts to gain control of the organization and administration of clerical revenue likewise failed and the *Juzgado* continued to function under the independent management of its officials. The several laws designed to restrict the lending activities achieved only a very limited success for a short period, because the State was not sufficiently organized or powerful to implement controversial legislation, particularly when the latter might affect the many borrowers of pious funds. The *Juzgado* fulfilled an essential need for farmers, merchants, and businessmen, and until its activities could be replaced by civil banks and credit institutions the State could take no effective action against it. Hence the *Juzgado* survived intact the turbulent years following independence, and it was only when the Church as a whole was forced by Juárez to acknowledge the supreme authority of the State that the lending and investment policy of the clergy was destroyed.

[1] Dublán y Lozano, III, 169–73.   [2] *Ibid.* 176–9, and IV, 6–9.

# CONCLUSION

The myriad activities and interests of the *Juzgado* clearly indicate its importance and influence within the economic and social structure of Mexico. As the sole banking institution in the country, the fiscal policy and lending operations undertaken by the various Judges and officials provided a unique source of finance for any aspiring merchant or impecunious landowner. To the latter, the Church must indeed have seemed benevolent, for the low interest charges and easy terms imposed by the clergy contrasted sharply with the exorbitant demands of the capitalist money-lenders, the notorious *agiotistas*. The *Juzgado* was not in the modern sense a profit-making enterprise. It owed its existence partly to the desire of the wealthy, for religious or other reasons, to bequeath money for the benefit of the Church or their descendants, and partly to the constant need of the property-owning classes to borrow money. Having achieved a substantial revenue the success of its operations was not determined by any preconceived policy or by the great spiritual influence of the Church, but by the public demand for financial assistance.

It was for this reason that the *Juzgado*, and to a lesser extent the regular orders, were allowed by the Spanish monarchy to achieve such extensive control of real estate by means of mortgages. The Crown had in effect no means of preventing this, for the public demand had to be met. The Church, as the bishop of Puebla pointed out in 1829, was in an ideal position to provide the required banking service. Its own internal organization was well established and the clergy themselves were the best educated section of society, with long experience and knowledge of fiscal matters. Furthermore, as far as the many benefactors could foresee, the Church was the only corporation which could be safely considered permanent and perpetual, and to which a rich man could entrust his wealth in the secure knowledge that his wishes concerning it would be respected. No civil body in the country was in a position to offer such a guarantee, nor to provide the personnel and expertise needed to manage the large amounts of capital involved. Any civil banking institution, even if non profit-making, would have had to demand adequate security for the funds which it lent to farmers and merchants. In a predominantly agrarian economy the only acceptable security was inevitably real estate. The public demand for loans coincided with the Church's own need to utilize its continuous, and in the colonial period increasing, flow of revenue, and therefore the clergy developed their lending policy.

Their only concern and duty was that the pious funds should be safeguarded to the greatest possible extent. They did not seek to make an excessive profit and originally determined the interest rate according to the yield which was required from the principal. When the cost of living increased and *capellanes* began to find their income insufficient, the Church did not raise the interest charges, but instead encouraged the founders of new benefices to increase the capital to be invested. Hence the interest remained constant, in spite of obvious pressures and circumstances conducive to a higher rate. The Church was not accused of usury because its interest charges were below the theoretical maximum of 6 per cent prescribed by the civil law. There is no evidence to indicate that it was pursuing some deliberate fiscal policy designed to secure economic and subsequently political control of the nation. The Judges and officials carried on the business according to the wishes or needs of the public, both benefactors and borrowers. The economic power wielded by the *Juzgado* at the beginning of the independence period was more the chance result than the deliberate intention of the Church.

The extent of the *Juzgado's* influence on the property-owning and middle classes is almost incalculable. Within the archbishopric, certainly the greater part of all real estate seems to have been mortgaged to it or to another of the ecclesiastical corporations. Indeed, documentary records, which contain thousands of requests for loans, reveal that much of the small industry which Alamán made such efforts to stimulate was dependent on the *Juzgado* for investment and even working capital. The same situation was repeated in every other diocese but unfortunately no study has yet been made of the activities of each *Juzgado*. We do not know if the contracts and terms imposed in other parts of the country were the same as those in the metropolitan see. Presumably in the mining areas many of the borrowers would be the mine-owners, but as this industry was in decline during the nineteenth century, and even at the best of times was a speculative venture, it seems likely that the Church will have varied the conditions concerning the security. The amount of the individual loans may also have been greater, but on the other hand in the more remote areas such as Durango the amounts must have been smaller because the bishopric was comparatively poor. Even in Durango, however, it was reported in 1856 that there was scarcely a house or farm that was not pledged to the Church. In the richer sees, for example Puebla and Michoacán, the *Juzgado*'s influence was probably as extensive as in the archdiocese. Abad y Queipo wrote that he himself had been the head of the *Juzgado* in Michoacán for twenty-two years. He estimated that of the two hundred thousand persons engaged in business of all kinds in New Spain, scarcely 20 per cent owned their working capital. The greater part of the latter had been borrowed from the Church. Agriculture, industry, and commerce were completely dependent on the pious funds.

In every State, therefore, the economic life of the region was dependent upon the successful operation of the *Juzgados*. The activities of these were in turn determined by the general position of the Church as a whole, for the Judges could only lend money if they received it in bequests and gifts. If the overall religious and spiritual influence of the Church declined, then this would result in fewer legacies and ecclesiastical benefices, with the result that they would have fewer funds to invest. This is in fact what took place in the nineteenth century, and the decline in the fortunes of the *Juzgados* was a direct reflection of the declining power of the Church as a whole.

There are several minor indications of this decline in the archbishopric. The considerable decrease in revenue as compared to the eighteenth century probably had the most significant effects. Personal loans of very large amounts could no longer be made and real estate became an essential security, whereas previously in many cases a few personal guarantors were sufficient. The borrowers after independence often had to wait some time for their loans because no money was available, and each prospective applicant was subjected, as were the terms of his proposal, to the detailed scrutiny of the Fiscal. In the later colonial period it had been easier to obtain a loan because capital was more abundant and readily available. A constant theme in the reports of the Judge's advisers was the need to take care with the pious funds and to ensure that they were invested safely. These and other points, such as the abolition of the Indian interpreter's post and the statement of the bishop of Puebla that nobody of common sense would establish a *capellanía* in the circumstances prevailing after independence, all clearly indicate that the position of the *Juzgado* was gradually weakening. The best example of the declining influence of the Church as a whole is provided by the tithes and the fact that once the civil obligation to pay them had ceased, few people could be persuaded to do so in spite of the constant appeals and threats of the clergy.

These separate minor factors all point to a weakening of the Church in the nineteenth century. After 1821 the clergy no longer formed the privileged corporation which enjoyed royal protection and support. The ecclesiastical *fuero*, although still in force, had been greatly reduced. The Judge in the *Juzgado* no longer had exclusive jurisdiction over disputes involving pious funds, and testamentary cases were now heard in the civil courts. Even the Tithe Judges had to go to the civil courts if they wished to take legal action against reluctant payers. Even more important was the shortage of clergy, which affected every diocese in the country. Many parishes remained vacant for years and in 1835 the Minister of Justice reported that the numbers of ecclesiastics was still decreasing. He feared that in some areas such as Durango, Monterey, and Sonora, there would soon not be a single priest in a very large part of the territory. In 1810 there had been more than four thousand secular clergy but by 1835 this had decreased to less than three thousand. According to the figures issued annually by the Ministry of Justice, in only one year between 1826 and 1851 were more than three-quarters of the parishes served by a priest. In some years, for example, 1828, 1829, 1830, 1843, almost half were vacant. The higher ranks of the clergy were in a similar position and not only was there an acute shortage of bishops but also the Cathedral chapters were greatly reduced in strength, that of the metropolitan see having only four members in 1833, instead of a possible complement of more than twenty.

It is not surprising that support for the Church among the population in general should have lost its original fervour. The rise to political prominence of the anticlerical radicals both reflected and contributed to this decline. During the first four decades of independence the liberals in their constant attacks on the Church did not immediately achieve their main objectives, for example the disamortization of ecclesiastical wealth, but they did gradually diminish the influence of the clergy. They contributed in part to the creation of a situation and an atmosphere in which clerical reform became a necessity, both on religious and economic grounds. The continuous political upheaval, the serious shortage of capital, the poverty of the national treasury, and the supposed ill-effects of Church investment and financial holdings, all made reform inevitable.

By 1856 some members of the clergy seem to have begun to accept the point of view of the liberals that the effects of Church wealth on the economy were detrimental. Thus the famous *Ley Lerdo*, promulgated on 25 June 1856, by which all ecclesiastical property was to be transferred to private ownership, was not universally condemned. The bishop of Guadalajara was said to support the measure, and even the Archbishop of Mexico, Lázaro de la Garza y Ballesteros, was believed to be in favour, although he refused to accept it without papal approval to do so.[1] It is perhaps indicative of the changing attitude that for the first time since independence a law which deprived the Church of its property was put into effect with considerable success. Nevertheless, the majority of the clergy adopted the traditional attitude and denounced the law. In the civil war which followed, the defeat of the conservative and pro-clerical forces led to the implementation of the liberal programme which had been basically formulated almost thirty years earlier in the period 1833–4. Ecclesiastical wealth

[1] Callcott, *Church and State...*, pp. 251–2.

was nationalized and the capital and revenue of the *Juzgado* became the property of the State. The disastrous effects of forcing the immediate redemption of all loans were avoided by granting the borrowers easy terms and long periods in which to pay their debts. The vacuum created by the disappearance of the *Juzgado* as the only effective banking institution in the country was filled by the establishment of civil banks, the first of these being the Bank of London and Mexico which opened in Mexico City in 1864.

# LIST OF SOURCES AND WORKS CITED

## PRINTED BIBLIOGRAPHIES

Castañeda, C. E., y Dabbs, J. A., *Guide to the Latin American Manuscripts in the University of Texas Library*. Harvard University Press, 1939.

*The Economic Literature of Latin America*. Bureau for Economic Research in Latin America, Harvard University. 2 vols., Cambridge, Mass., 1935–6.

*Handbook of Latin American Studies*. Harvard University Press, 1936–50; University of Florida Press 1951– .

Humphreys, R. A. *Latin American History. A Guide to the Literature in English*. Oxford, 1958.

Ker, A. M. *Mexican Government Publications. A Guide to the more Important Publications of the National Government of Mexico, 1821–1936*. Washington, 1940.

Millares Carlo, A. *Repertorio bibliográfico de los archivos mexicanos y de los europeos y norteamericanos de interés para la historia de México*. Mexico, 1959.

Ramos, R. *Bibliografía de la historia de México*. Mexico, 1956.

Sánchez Alonso, B. *Fuentes de la historia española e hispanoamericana*. 3rd ed., 3 vols., Madrid, 1952.

## MANUSCRIPT SOURCES

Most of the information gathered for this study has been found in the Archivo General de la Nación Mexico City. In particular, the following sections have been consulted:

| | |
|---|---|
| Capellanías | Justicia Eclesiástica |
| Clero Regular y Secular | Obispos y Arzobispos |
| Diezmos | Papeles de Bienes Nacionales |
| Historia | Templos y Conventos |

The Archivo Histórico de Hacienda has also been used, particularly sections:

Donativos y Préstamos
Justicia Eclesiástica

The metropolitan chapter archives, housed at present in the Cathedral, have retained almost no documents pertaining to the *Juzgado*. This source, however, was found to be invaluable for details on tithes and on Church–State relations during the nineteenth century.

133

One other archive has been used to fill an important gap in the records of the *Juzgado*. This is the Archivo de Notarías, Mexico City. Whenever the *Juzgado* made a loan, a contract was drawn up by a public notary to be signed by the representatives of the Church as creditor, and by the borrower. Two copies, in addition to the original, were made of each contract, one being deposited in the archive of the *Juzgado*, and the other being given to the borrower. In spite of the fact that many thousands of these contracts were made, with few exceptions the copies which should have been among the bulk of the *Juzgado*'s records in the Archivo General have disappeared. On the final page of each expediente dealing with a loan, however, it was customary to note the date on which the contract was signed and also the name of the public notary concerned. Armed with these essential facts it is possible to locate some of the original contracts drawn up by the various notaries, whose papers and records are now in the Archivo de Notarías

### WORKS CITED

Full details of works relevant to the history of Mexico, including ecclesiastical affairs, will be found in the bibliographies listed above, although I have been unable to locate any direct and accurate reference to the *Juzgado*. The following list, therefore, contains only those works to which reference has been made in the text.

Abad y Queipo, M. 'Representación a nombre de los labradores y comerciantes de Valladolid de Michoacán, en que se demuestran con claridad los gravísimos inconvenientes de que se ejecute en las Américas la real cédula de 26 de diciembre de 1804, sobre enajenación de bienes raíces y cobro de capitales de capellanías y obras pías para la consolidación de vales', 24 October 1805; published in G. B. Castillo, *Estudios de Abad y Queipo*. Mexico, 1947.

Alamán, L. *Historia de México desde los primeros movimientos que prepararon su independencia en el año de 1808 hasta la época presente.* 5 vols., Mexico, 1849–52.

Alfaro y Piña, L. *Relación descriptiva de la fundación de las iglesias y conventos de México.* Mexico, 1863.

Arrillaga, B. *Cartas por B. Arrillaga al Dr. Mora citándole a responder por los fundamentos y resultados de sus opiniones sobre bienes eclesiásticos, producidas en el tomo primero de sus obras sueltas.* Mexico, 1839.

Callcott, W. H. *Church and State in Mexico, 1822–1857.* Durham, N. Carolina, 1926.

# Sources

Chevalier, F. *Land and Society in Colonial Mexico*. California, 1963.

*Colección eclesiástica mexicana*. 4 vols., Mexico, 1834.

*Correo de la Federación Mexicana*, 26 February 1829.

Costeloe, M. P. 'Guide to the chapter archives of the archbishopric of Mexico', *Hispanic American Historical Review*, XLV (Feb. 1965), 53–63.

——'The Mexican Church and the rebellion of the Polkos', *Hispanic American Historical Review*, XLVI (May 1966), 170–8.

——'The administration, collection and distribution of tithes in the archbishopric of Mexico, 1800–1860', *The Americas*, XXIII (July 1966), 3–27.

——'Church–State financial negotiations in Mexico during the American war, 1846–1847', *Revista de Historia de América*, 60 (June–December 1965).

Cuevas, M. *Historia de la Iglesia en México*. 5th ed., 5 vols., Mexico, 1947.

*Diario del Gobierno*, 30 September 1843, 22 January 1847.

Dublán, M., y Lozano, J. M. *Legislación mexicana*. Vols. I–IV, Mexico, 1876.

*El Católico*, 30 January 1847.

'Enfermedades políticas que padece la capital de esta Nueva España en casi todos los cuerpos de que se compone; y remedios que se la deben aplicar para su curación si se quiere que sea útil al público' (20 May 1785), published in *Voz de la Patria*, suppl. no. 1, 11 September 1830.

*Estado de las fincas urbanas y rústicas respectivas a las temporalidades de los ecs-jesuitas y monacales suprimidas, con expresión de sus valores, gravamen que reportan y renta anual*. Mexico, 1829.

*Exposición dirigida al congreso general por la Comisión de Acreedores al camino de Perote a Veracruz pidiendo no se comprendan en las medidas propuestas por la Comisión de Crédito Público de la cámara de diputados, las hipotecas del peage y la avería que especialmente están consignadas a los mismos acreedores*. Mexico, 1849.

*Exposición que el Provincial del Carmen hizo al Supremo Gobierno sobre las ventas de fincas que celebraron algunos conventos de su orden*. Mexico, 1834.

*Exposición que la legislatura del estado libre y soberano de México eleva a la cámara de diputados sobre el decreto de 3 de enero de este año sobre redención de capitales piadosos, precedida de los documentos respectivos*. Toluca, 1849.

*Exposición que los acreedores al fondo dotal de minería elevan a la augusta cámara de diputados en defensa de sus derechos*. Mexico, 1849.

Galarza, E. *The Roman Catholic Church as a Factor in the Political and Social History of Mexico*. Sacramento, 1928.

Galván Rivera, M. *Concilio III Mexicano, celebrado en México el año de 1585*. Mexico, 1859.

Guzmán, M. L. (ed.). *Leyes de reforma*. 2nd ed., Mexico, 1955.

Hale, C. A. 'José María Luis Mora and the structure of Mexican liberalism', *Hispanic American Historical Review*, XLV (May 1965).

Hernández, O. A. *Esquema de la economía mexicana hasta antes de la revolución*. Mexico, 1961.

Humboldt, A. von (trans. J. Black). *Political Essay on the Kingdom of New Spain*. 4 vols., London, 1811.

*La Cruz*, 8 November 1855, 22 July 1858.

López, E. L. *El crédito en México*. Mexico, 1945.

*Memoria del Ministro de Justicia y Negocios Eclesiásticos*, 1825, 1826, 1828.

*Memoria del Ministro de Hacienda*, 1870.

Mora, J. M. L. *Disertación sobre la naturaleza y aplicación de las rentas y bienes eclesiasticos (1834)*. Mexico, 1957.

——*El clero, el estado y la economía nacional*, ed. M. L. Guzmán. Mexico, 1950.

——'La agricultura nacional; estado de bancarrota a que se halla reducida', *Boletín de Agricultura*. Mexico, 1846.

Parra, P. *La sociología de la reforma*. Mexico, 1948.

*Periódico oficial del supremo gobierno de los estados unidos mexicanos*, 22 June 1850.

Phipps, H. 'Some aspects of the agrarian question in Mexico', *University of Texas Bulletin*, no. 2515. Austin, 1925.

Potash, R. A. *El Banco de Avío de México. El fomento de la industria, 1821–1846*. Mexico, 1959.

Quirós, J. M. *Memoria de estatuto. Causas de que ha procedido que la agricultura, industria y minería de Nueva España no hayan adquirido el gran fomento de que son susceptibles. Medidas que contribuirán que restablezcan de la ruina que les ha ocasionado la insurección de sus provincias*. Mexico, 1818.

Shiels, W. E. 'Church and State in the first decade of Mexican independence', *Catholic Historical Review*, XXVIII (July 1942).

Sierra, J. *México. Su evolución social*. 3 vols., Mexico, 1902.

Toro, A. *La iglesia y el estado en México*. Mexico, 1927.

Vera, F. H. *Legislación eclesiástica mexicana*. Vol. III, Amecameca, 1887.

Ward, H. G. *Mexico in 1827*. 2 vols., London, 1828.

Zamacois, N. de. *Historia de México*. Barcelona, 1878–88, vol. XV.

Zavala, L. de. *Ensayo histórico de las revoluciones de México, desde 1808 hasta 1830*. 2 vols., Mexico, 1845.

# INDEX

# Index